CREATIVE
HOME DESIGN

ROOMS FOR EVERYDAY LIVING

CREATIVE HOME DESIGN

ROOMS FOR EVERYDAY LIVING

Rima A. Suqi ✦ Lisa Skolnik ✦ Barbara B. Buchholz

BARNES
&NOBLE
BOOKS
NEW YORK

A BARNES & NOBLE BOOK

©1999 by Michael Friedman Publishing Group, Inc.

All rights reserved. No part of this publication may be reproduced,
stored in a retrieval system, or transmitted, in any form or by any means,
electronic, mechanical, photocopying, recording, or otherwise,
without prior written permission from the publisher.

ISBN 0-7607-4626-5

Editors: Reka Simonsen and Hallie Einhorn
Art Directors: Jeff Batzli and Lynne Yeamans
Designers: Charles Donahue, Tanya Ross-Hughes, Jennifer S. Markson, and Jan Melchior
Photography Editors: Jennifer Bove, Wendy Missan, and Emilya Naymark
Production Director: Karen Matsu Greenberg
Production Associates: Ingrid McNamara and Camille Lee

Color separations by Fine Arts Repro House Co. Ltd.
Printed in China by Leefung-Asco Printers Ltd.

1 3 5 7 9 10 8 6 4 2

Table of Contents

INTRODUCTION

A hundred years ago, the late Victorians lived in fussy homes filled with furnishings and decorated with details from myriad periods and places. Their parlors, drawing rooms, dining rooms, and libraries were crammed full of elaborate furniture and cluttered with eclectic collections and objets d'art. But their kitchens and washrooms were spartan affairs devoted solely to function, while the concept of an informal dining area or a home office was so foreign that the notion would probably seem shocking to anyone of that day.

In reality, the Victorians' homes were a reflection of the times. Thanks to the Industrial Revolution, there was a growing middle class with some wealth, and their homes became vehicles for displaying experiences, accomplishments, and travels. Though dark (they abhorred natural light), ornate, and incredibly excessive by today's standards, these houses were havens of comfort and convention that reflected the Victorian lifestyle and psyche.

A century later, our homes still reflect the times. And though it seems unlikely, we have many similarities to the Victorians. Thanks to mass communication and rampant wanderlust, we revel in glories both ancient and exotic, and we freely integrate our passions into our

Opposite: KITCHENS HAVE CERTAINLY COME A LONG WAY SINCE THE NINETEENTH CENTURY, WHEN THEY WERE DESIGNED FOR FOOD PREPARATION ALONE, AND COULD ONLY ACCOMMODATE ONE COOK. THIS SPACIOUS KITCHEN HAS ROOM FOR SEVERAL PEOPLE TO WORK AND A LONG ISLAND THAT PROVIDES A PLACE FOR FRIENDS TO SIT AND CHAT WITH THE COOK, OR JUST SAMPLE THE GOODIES. **Above:** THIS PRISTINE BATHROOM HAS THE SIMPLICITY AND PURE WHITE COLOR SCHEME OF A TYPICAL VICTORIAN BATH, BUT IT IS MUCH MORE WELCOMING. PERSONAL TOUCHES SUCH AS THE POTTED PLANTS, PLUSH TOWELS, WHIMSICAL FRAMED DRAWING, AND BLINDS THAT ALLOW IN SPLASHES OF SUN MAKE ALL THE DIFFERENCE.

homes. Spaces today are filled with furnishings, are decorated with details from many periods and places, and, most significantly, reveal our lifestyles and psyches. But the similarities stop there. After all, we've come a long, long way in a hundred years.

During the twentieth century, we have witnessed the rise of interior design as a profession, with Elsie de Wolfe, who nabbed her first official job in 1905, claiming to be the first real decorator. This helped fuel a roller coaster of styles that took us from the excess of the Victorian era to the stark simplicity of modernism by mid-century and back to excess again by the end of the 1980s. In the nineties, the pendulum swung back to a simpler, more modest mode, but today we still pay homage to the history-rich twentieth century by reviving or evoking various styles that have been played out during the past hundred years.

We have also witnessed a new sort of industrial revolution in the twentieth century, thanks to the invention of the microchip. With such innovations as personal computers, productivity software, modems, fax machines, voice mail, and electronic mail, not only has working at home become easy and efficient, it is now de rigueur—most of us do it in one form or another.

So what has been the effect of these forces? Nothing short of monumental changes in the way we live. Consider the typical home: in recent years it has undergone a massive transformation and now looks substantially different than it did even a decade ago.

The once humble and solely utilitarian washroom has undergone a metamorphosis, emerging larger, and much more lavish, than ever before. Now the simple washroom invariably sports interesting and often exotic trappings, while bathrooms contain much more than just the tub that lends them their name.

Kitchens have gone from modest spaces for preparing meals to large, airy rooms that are multifunctional and "zoned" for all sorts of tasks, be they cooking, eating, or even office work. Living and dining rooms have shrunk and been displaced by the expansive and all-encompassing great room, which usually houses a whole assortment of audiovisual equipment and often has distinct areas for reading, relaxing, and dining.

Home offices have become an entire domain unto themselves, for everyone either wants one or has one. After all, it is hard to resist the lure of a thirty-second commute, tailor-made hours, and permanent casual days. The popularity of this room has fueled a whole new industry that revolves around an expanding and evolving array of furniture and equipment. The possibilities for a home office are endless, which adds to the allure: it can be anything from a sensible, nuts-and-bolts setup to a dressed-up space designed to the nines.

So if the truth be told, bathrooms, kitchens, dining areas, and offices have now become perhaps the most important and frequently used spaces in our homes. Fueled by the imagination, ingenuity, and requirements of this generation of homeowners, these spaces have taken on infinite forms as we lavish them with attention and direct our resources their way. The results have been nothing short of astonishing, as these rooms embrace every style in the spectrum and fulfill a panoply of needs.

This begs the question "What does all this mean?" Are we living any differently than we ever have, and does it really signify anything? In fact, many professionals in the home design industry as well as scholars who chronicle and analyze our times think there's a new order afoot. And by their reckoning, our homes are indeed a tool for analysis, a notion suggested and substantiated by the French philosopher Gaston Bachelard in his groundbreaking 1958 tome *The Poetics of Space.*

According to the consulting firm Yankelovich Partners, which tracks social change and trends across

Above: HOW MANY PEOPLE CAN BOAST OF AN OFFICE WITH A WATERFRONT VIEW? IN ADDITION TO BETTER SCENERY, HOME OFFICES PROVIDE MANY PERQUISITES THAT CORPORATE OFFICES RARELY DO: NATURAL LIGHTING, ADEQUATE STORAGE SPACE, AND A WORK AREA THAT IS TAILORED TO YOUR SPECIFIC NEEDS. THIS LOVELY SPACE ALSO INCORPORATES A SKYLIGHT TO TAKE FULL ADVANTAGE OF THE OPEN SKY AND BRIGHT DAYLIGHT.

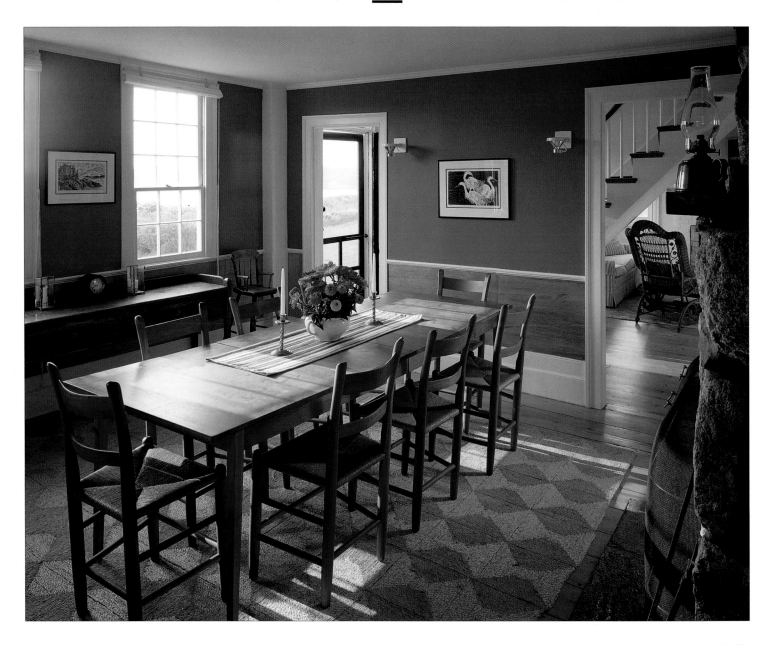

Above: THIS GORGEOUS DINING AREA HAS OPEN DOORWAYS LEADING TO THE LIVING ROOM, WHICH GIVES IT THE AIRINESS AND COMFORT OF A GREAT ROOM. THE WARM, EARTHY HUES OF HONEY, WHEAT, AND CLAY CREATE A PEACEFUL ENVIRONMENT CONDUCIVE TO RELAXED MEALS AND GOOD CONVERSATION. DELICATE ETCHINGS OF THE NEARBY OCEAN AND ITS FAUNA STRENGTHEN THE ROOM'S CONNECTION WITH NATURE.

America, basically all we want our homes to be boils down to the three Cs: comfortable, casual, and cozy. The home is a place to relax, unwind, and have fun, and has become less of a showplace and more of an environment that really suits us.

Is this really so different than it ever was? Surprisingly, yes. Much like the Victorians, we once viewed our homes as both a showplace and a major investment. But we look at things differently these days. In the early nineties, we started seeing our homes as a return on enjoyment rather than merely a return on an investment. And this tendency is growing stronger. Our focus is now on our relationships with our places rather than the eventual payback when we move on.

And in any relationship, there are ground rules. But those very precepts are also changing. Gone are the days of all those rigid decrees about how to furnish and decorate our homes. Being proper and appropriate is a moot point. There's no right way to do it, no edicts that dictate what a home has to have. Instead, we prefer to live in homes that reflect our wants and needs—and look pretty good, too.

This explains why the rooms we once coveted have become less important and why spaces we never even conceived of as being consequential—such as bathrooms, kitchens, dining areas, and home offices—are now such integral parts of our lives. These are rooms to which we now devote lots of attention. But since our lifestyles are so complex today, this can often lead to a lengthy and evolving decorating process that changes as we do.

Any decorating process is inspired by new concepts, which is why this volume takes a close look at these four now-significant spaces. On the following pages, you will find an array of practical and imaginative ideas to help

you make your own versions of these spaces stylish, serviceable, and an integral part of your home.

Above: THIS CHARMING WINDOW SEAT TURNS INTO A DINING NOOK WITH THE ADDITION OF A ROUND DROP-LEAF TABLE. THE BEAUTIFUL VIEW AND FRESH BREEZES MAKE THIS A PERFECT SPOT FOR CASUAL BRUNCHES, CONVERSATIONS ACCOMPANIED BY HOT TEA AND COOKIES, OR CURLING UP WITH A JUST-PICKED APPLE AND A GOOD BOOK.

PART ONE
BATHROOMS

INTRODUCTION

Ask most homeowners which room is at the top of their wish list to decorate or remodel, and often they'll say it is the bathroom, the most functional and personal space in the home.

Part of the urge is based on pure economics. Unlike adding a swimming pool or redoing a basement recreation room, a refurbished bathroom brings one of the greatest returns for the money invested.

But money provides just part of the explanation. Some of our current fascination with sprucing up and remodeling bathrooms is due to the relative youthfulness of the room as a full-fledged member of a typical home's layout. The bathroom is the new kid on the block. As an indoor space consisting of a sink (called a lavatory in the industry), a tub, and a toilet, it dates back less than one hundred years.

Through much of history, even polite folk had only two less-than-ideal choices: because there was no such thing as indoor plumbing, they could use an outhouse or a chamber pot. For cleansing, they often ventured to their local public baths where they bathed communally, albeit sometimes in luxurious settings.

The first American sink, whose predecessor was a pitcher and basin set on a washstand, dates from the

Opposite: BATHED IN PALE NEUTRAL TONES, THIS CONTEMPORARY BATHROOM HAS A REFINED LOOK THAT IS SOOTHING TO THE EYE. MIRRORS RESEMBLING HALF MOONS ARE A WELCOME SURPRISE ON THE MEDICINE-CABINET DOORS AND PROVIDE THE ENTIRE SPACE WITH A FRESH, ORIGINAL LOOK. **Above:** TO ACHIEVE A BOLD CONTEMPORARY TONE, AN ANGLED STAINLESS STEEL VANITY WAS PLACED AGAINST A WALL OF GLASS BLOCKS AND OUTFITTED WITH A HIGH-NECKED FAUCET THAT DISPLAYS LABORATORYLIKE SLEEKNESS. FRESH FLOWERS SOFTEN THE STARKNESS—JUST A BIT.

mid-1800s, when sanitary sewers were installed and indoor running water became possible. Credit for this advance is given to Philadelphia architect John Notman, who supplied a home with water via a hydraulic ramp. John Michael Kohler, founder of the huge plumbing conglomerate Kohler Co., sold his first tub to a farmer in 1883. And the first American firm to introduce a vitreous china tank toilet was Eljer Plumbingware Co. in 1907.

But it was not until later in the twentieth century that the bathroom with all three fixtures became part of the typical home. Such a room was usually quite small. At first, not much heed was paid to showcasing the fixtures in more than the most utilitarian way.

The idea of giving a bathroom a distinct style and all the trappings of other rooms did not emerge until the 1920s and '30s, at which point such decorating was done mostly by the wealthy, many of whom were captivated by the large, glamorous bathrooms that Hollywood producers showed in their films. Decades later, after World War II and as suburbs burgeoned nationwide, a larger segment of the population began to enjoy the amenities of the bathroom. The growing demand gave rise to innovations. In 1968, inventor Roy Jacuzzi introduced his now-famous tub with water jets,

which was followed by a wave of step-up and step-down whirlpool bathtubs.

Another element that has inspired large numbers of homeowners to refurbish their bathrooms is the fitness and health craze of the last two decades. This trend has created a demand for appealing spots in which to clean up after a workout, particularly among adults with master bathrooms, which lend themselves to being transformed into pampering retreats.

For these rooms, shower manufacturers have copycatted whirlpool designers and debuted larger and more extravagant shower stalls, complete with a variety of showerheads, body sprays, and nozzles. Such showers are often enclosed in sculptural glass-wall designs to provide the feeling of bathing outdoors. The result is a therapeutic relaxation center.

Some homeowners have also come to favor the incorporation of multiple fixtures, the advantages of which they already discovered in their well-equipped kitchens. The goal is similar: to allow two people to use the space simultaneously.

The most lavish of these examples are equivalent to full-size, fully furnished rooms. They boast exercise equipment; comfortable seating; good natural and

Left: ALTHOUGH TILES ARE AMONG THE MOST COMMONLY USED MATERIALS IN BATHROOMS, THEY HAVE THE ABILITY TO CREATE DESIGNS THAT ARE FAR FROM ORDINARY. HERE, A JUMBLE OF MANY TYPES OF TILES BRINGS EXCITEMENT TO A POWDER ROOM, DESPITE A SUBDUED PALETTE. THREE DIFFERENT KINDS OF SCULPTURED BORDER TILES PROVIDE DEPTH AND TEXTURE AS THEY OUTLINE THE SINK AND TRIM THE OVERHANG. LARGER TILES— SOME STRAIGHT UP AND DOWN, SOME ON THE DIAGONAL—COVER THE REST OF THE SPACE, THEIR DIFFERENT HUES AND DIFFERENT POSITIONS DEFYING PREDICTABILITY.

Above: WITH THE HELP OF TROMPE L'OEIL WALLPAPER, THIS CHARMING POWDER ROOM WAS DESIGNED TO LOOK LIKE A BOOK-LINED RETREAT WHERE ONE WOULD WANT TO LINGER. COMBINED WITH A TAFFETA BALLOON SHADE AND AN ANTIQUE STOOL, THE FAUX LEATHER-BOUND VOLUMES GIVE THE ROOM AN OLD-FASHIONED FEELING.

artificial lighting; large windows; abundant storage in medicine cabinets, under vanities, and in closets; and such other amenities as heated towel racks, telephones, televisions, stereo systems, and mirrors equipped with anti-fogging devices.

But master bathrooms are not the only ones targeted for fixing up. Less private bathrooms such as powder rooms or half-bathrooms (often located near a front entry hall or by a kitchen or mudroom), children's bathrooms, and guest bathrooms have followed suit. Even new types of bathrooms have emerged, such as the outdoor bathroom, which consists of a showerhead to wash off sand or dirt and sometimes a soaking tub.

Manufacturers have taken advantage of people's interest in decorating bathrooms by offering fixtures, tiles, wallpapers, and floorings in a plethora of styles, sizes, and colors. They even supply such accessories as soap dishes, toothbrush holders, wastepaper baskets, hooks, and scales in a wide variety of incarnations.

Many of the materials, patterns, and colors have been influenced by trends in other home furnishings. When the lean industrial look took hold in the 1970s, hospital scrub sinks, stainless steel counters, and doctor's cabinets started popping up in home bathrooms. When an interest in the Orient materialized in the 1980s, Japanese-style teak soaking tubs became de rigueur in Far Eastern–inspired bathrooms.

The trend now is clearly not toward a single look, but for designs that share some common denominators with the rest of the home's decor. Bathrooms have become as varied in their style, mood, and size as any other room in the home. Some are quite elegant, with marble floors and antique mirrors to rival the most opulent Roman baths, while others are downright contemporary and funky, with crayon-colored faucets and a rainbow of different-colored tiles covering the walls and floors.

Other bathrooms reflect their settings or owners' interests. A bathroom for a beach house may have tiles with a seashell motif, permanently sunny yellow towels, and soaps shaped like fish. A young child's bathroom may have smaller fixtures complemented by wallpaper borders that teach how to count or to recognize the letters of the alphabet. And the bathroom of a plant aficionado may house a conservatory of greens because the humidity helps certain varieties, such as ferns, thrive.

Not all bathrooms are large and elaborate, however. Some are actually quite small—almost as tiny as those on airplanes and trains. Often, they are made to look larger with mirrors placed on the walls and ceilings.

Decorating a bathroom can be relatively easy these days, thanks to many new and affordable bathroom resources, such as neighborhood design and hardware centers, home furnishings mail-order catalogs, and salvage shops. You may find the perfect antique claw-foot tub and pedestal sink for a fraction of their original value because someone decided they just had to have a computer-programmed whirlpool tub that would allow them to turn on their bathwater while still at the office.

Although redoing a bathroom can exceed many families' budgets, the process need not be so expensive. The secret is to set priorities: decide what you can reuse, what you should discard, and what new features and fixtures you view as most important.

Small Spaces

Not all bathrooms have become large and ultraluxurious. Indeed, the small bathroom remains a necessity in many homes on account of space constraints. Due to the small size of these rooms, a great deal of imagination is often necessary to incorporate all the basic features and to make the spaces look larger and more appealing. The challenge becomes even greater when ceilings are angled because of sloping roof lines and when walls jut out creating nooks and crannies, though such architectural elements can be played up to add charm and whimsy.

The smallest type of bathroom has traditionally been the powder room, which is also referred to as a half-bathroom because it excludes a tub. Such rooms are sometimes fashioned out of former closets or from space borrowed from other rooms. Often, the sink and toilet are scaled down in size so that they will fit into the compact space. The smaller scale of these rooms, though, does not mean that they have to be any less attractive than their larger counterparts. In fact, many demonstrate a tremendous amount of ingenuity. And they come in all different styles, from casual to dressy, depending on the location in the home and the rest of the decor.

Those bathrooms adjacent to the front hallway are often rather formal, showing off fancy paint finishes or wallpapers, as well as elegant marble or wood floors. Small bathrooms near the kitchen, back hall, or family room, however, are often designed to sustain harder wear and tear, so they tend to have floors, wall coverings, and accessories of a more practical nature.

Opposite: Framed black-and-white photographs of celebrities accent one wall in a film buff's powder room. A large mirror duplicates the favorite images and expands the tiny space, which is outfitted with a small pedestal sink and a sturdy but basic schoolroom-type armchair that serves as an extra towel rack. The walls are painted with a crackle finish to suggest age. **Above:** Evoking the feeling of a garden, the walls in this bathroom were painted to resemble blocks of stone, then accented with painted trailing vines and flowers. Café curtains bearing a similar floral motif, a basket boasting a dried arrangement, and a framed botanical print contribute to the bucolic feeling. These finishing touches also add soothing bits of color to the mostly monochromatic space.

Left: THIS ANTIQUE STAINLESS STEEL BOWL, WHICH HAS MORE AESTHETIC THAN MONETARY VALUE, HAS TAKEN ON A NEW LIFE AS A SINK BASIN IN A POWDER ROOM. PAIRED WITH A STRIKINGLY CONTEMPORARY FAUCET AND PLACED ATOP AN OLD WOOD TABLE, THE BOWL IS PART OF AN ECLECTIC MIX THAT FORMS AN ATTRACTIVE THREE-DIMENSIONAL STILL LIFE.

Opposite: A CURVING CABINET CRAFTED FROM MAPLE WAS ELEVATED TO ART STATUS WHEN ITS FRONT WAS PAINTED WITH A ROMANESQUE-TYPE GARDEN DESIGN. THE MARBLE COUNTERTOP AND BACKSPLASH PICK UP THE DEEP GREEN-GRAY TONES, WHICH ARE ALSO ECHOED IN THE LEAFY BORDER OF THE MIRROR.

Opposite: BY ANGLING A SCALED-DOWN SINK IN A CORNER, THE OWNERS OF THIS INVITING HALL BATHROOM WERE ABLE TO SQUEEZE A TOILET INTO THE COMPACT SPACE. BRASS FIXTURES, GILT FRAMES, AND THE YELLOWISH BACKGROUND OF THE FLORAL-PATTERNED WALLPAPER AND MATCHING SINK SKIRT CAST A GOLDEN WARMTH UPON THE AREA. ACCENTED BY A CLASSIC BRASS CANDLESTICK AND A SMALL BOUQUET OF FRESH FLOWERS, THE ROOM HAS AN ALMOST ROMANTIC FEELING. THE USE OF A SOLID, DARK HUE ON THE DADO, CEILING, AND CURTAIN LINING PROVIDES A GROUNDING SENSE OF CONTRAST. **Above, left:** SOMETIMES A "BATHROOM" CAN CONSIST OF JUST A SINK IN A HALLWAY, AS IN THIS ALCOVE OFF A BEDROOM. AN OLD, PAINTED-WHITE WOODEN TABLE WAS GIVEN A NEW TOP, INTO WHICH A SIMPLE WHITE BOWL WAS PLACED. A MONOGRAMMED HAND TOWEL, AN OLD-FASHIONED TOWEL HOOK, A LARGE MIRROR, AND A VASE PERENNIALLY FILLED WITH FLOWERS ENHANCE THE ICONOCLASTIC SETTING. **Above, right:** UNORTHODOX IN ITS PAIRINGS, THIS POWDER ROOM BOLDLY DEFIES CONVENTION. SIDE MIRRORS FROM A TRUCK SCREAM MODERN SOCIETY WHILE ORNATE CRYSTAL CHANDELIERS HARKEN BACK TO A QUIETER TIME. THE LAVATORY, CONSISTING OF A LARGE, WHITE CHINA BOWL MOUNTED ATOP A MARBLE COUNTER RATHER THAN SUNK INTO IT, ALSO PRESENTS AN UNUSUAL TWIST. THE WALLS AND FLOOR WERE DELIBERATELY LEFT AS A MONOCHROMATIC EXPANSE SO AS NOT TO INTERFERE WITH THE UNIQUE COLLECTION OF FIXTURES AND DECORATIVE OBJECTS.

Above: Connoting cleanliness and freshness, the color white creates a wholesome air in this small wood-lined bathroom. Airy brackets resembling garden lattices further contribute to the natural feeling of the room, while at the same time serve the highly functional purpose of supporting necessary shelves. A collection of old blue and green bottles found at roadside shops rests on one of these shelves, adding a gentle splash of color to the surroundings. **Opposite:** Filled with a sense of nostalgia, this quaint washroom, carved out of a bedroom corner, boasts a china bowl and pitcher atop a painted wooden cabinet. Cheery blue-and-white striped ticking covers the base of the cabinet, giving the room a summery air year-round. Darker blue and white stripes flank the full-length mirror and grace the area rug, which feels comforting to bare feet on cold mornings. Above the mirror, a frieze from a demolished building adds panache.

Below: IN THIS TINY ATTIC BATHROOM, AN OLD WOODEN CABINET WAS FITTED TO HOUSE A SINK AND THEN TOPPED WITH A STONE SLAB, A SMALLER VERSION OF WHICH RESTS ATOP THE BACK OF THE PIECE. THE CASUAL MOOD OF THE ROOM WAS PLAYED UP BY USING A SIMPLE, OLD WOODEN MEDICINE CABINET, TERRA-COTTA FLOOR TILES, AND PALE SHADES OF PAINT. A GREEN LINE RUNNING ALONG THE WALL ECHOES THE SLOPE OF THE ROOF.

Opposite: A NARROW BATHROOM WITH FIFTIES-STYLE TILING WAS SPRUCED UP WITH MINIMAL EFFORT AND WITHOUT EXPENSIVE ARCHITECTURAL CHANGES BY INCORPORATING SOME HANDSOME YET SIMPLE PIECES INTO THE SPACE: A CRISP WHITE PEDESTAL SINK WITH DECKS AND TOWEL RACKS ON BOTH SIDES, A LARGE MIRROR WITH A FANCIFUL PAINTED CURLICUE DESIGN, A LARGE OVERSCALE WIRE WASTEBASKET, AND A RATTAN TABLE THAT SERVES AS A RESTING SPOT FOR EXTRA TOWELS AND FRESH BLOOMS. STARLIKE ACCENTS ON THE FLOOR JAZZ UP THE SPACE. **Above:** INSTEAD OF IGNORING THE STEEP PITCH OF THIS BATHROOM CEILING, THE DESIGNER USED IT TO HIS ADVANTAGE BY INTRODUCING AN ENORMOUS GEOMETRIC MIRROR THAT TAKES UP ALMOST THE ENTIRE WALL. THE HEXAGONAL SHAPE IS REPEATED IN THE SINK, WHICH IS COVERED WITH BLUE-TINTED GLASS THAT ECHOES THE DISPLAY SHELVES.

Above, left: THIS POWDER ROOM OFF A FRONT HALL DAZZLES GUESTS WITH ALL ITS GLITZ AND GLAMOUR. EXUDING OPULENCE, A BLACK MARBLE COUNTERTOP SITS REGALLY ATOP A RICHLY HUED MAHOGANY CABINET AND GRACEFULLY HOUSES A GOLD-TONED SINK. ADORNED BY BRASS-AND-CRYSTAL FIXTURES, THE SHINY SINK MAKES WASHING ONE'S HANDS SEEM LIKE A DECADENTLY LUXURIOUS AFFAIR. A GOLD-LEAFED MIRROR FLANKED BY ELEGANT SCONCES BECKONS THE VISITOR TO PRIMP, CREATING A CAPTIVATING FRAME FOR THE IMAGE IT REFLECTS. **Above, right:** THIS SMALL POWDER ROOM RECEIVES ITS UNUSUAL APPEAL VIA A COMBINATION OF DETAILS: A MATCHING SET OF OLD-FASHIONED FRAMES MADE OF WOOD AND TIN, A NARROW BACKSPLASH OF TRIANGULAR AND DIAMOND-SHAPED TILES IN SHADES OF ROSE AND GRAY, AND AN ANTIQUE JAPANESE BOWL THAT TAKES THE PLACE OF A TRADITIONAL BASIN. THE TRIANGULAR DESIGN OF THE COUNTERTOP, ECHOED BY THE ROSE TILES, IS AN EFFECTIVE MEANS OF SAVING SPACE. **Opposite:** HERE, AN OLD PEDESTAL WITH DEEP CARVINGS AND RELIEFS HAS BEEN TRANSFORMED INTO AN INNOVATIVE SINK THAT WILL KEEP GUESTS TALKING. SPORTING A HIGH-NECKED FAUCET, WHICH WAS OBTAINED FROM A HOSPITAL SUPPLY SOURCE, THE SINK HAS AN ELONGATED LOOK THAT MAKES THE REST OF THE ROOM SEEM LARGER. THIS SPATIAL ILLUSION IS FURTHER ENHANCED BY A FULL-LENGTH MIRROR POSITIONED STRATEGICALLY BEHIND THE SINK. MAHOGANY PANELING COVERS THE WALLS AND CEILING, ENVELOPING THE SPACE WITH A MAJESTIC TONE.

Opposite: IN SPITE OF ITS SMALL SIZE, THIS APARTMENT BATHROOM WAS GIVEN AN ELEGANT MAKEOVER. A SMALL ORIENTAL RUG WAS PLACED ON TOP OF THE ORIGINAL VINYL FLOOR; A GOTHIC-INSPIRED CHAIR WITH AN ELABORATE SEAT COVER WAS BROUGHT IN FOR APPLYING MAKEUP; AND A NARROW SET OF SHELVES WAS TUCKED INTO A CORNER TO KEEP FAVORITE PICTURES AND READING MATTER HANDY. SMALL PHOTOGRAPHS OF FAMOUS STATUES ARE DISPLAYED ARTFULLY AROUND THE ROOM, TRANSFORMING IT INTO A GALLERY OF SORTS. **Right:** BOASTING VIBRANT RED FLOWERS AGAINST A BLACK BACKGROUND, THE WALLPAPER IN THIS ORNATE POWDER ROOM MAKES A DRAMATIC STATEMENT. EQUALLY DRAMATIC ARE THE RICHLY CARVED GOLD MIRROR AND ELABORATE CRYSTAL CHANDELIER, WHICH GIVE THE SMALL SPACE A PALATIAL FEEL.

STYLE

The styles of bathrooms vary tremendously. There are those with a period look, incorporating fixtures that come from a certain country or time; contemporary spaces made to look old with the addition of antique claw-foot tubs and washstands; and ultramodern designs boasting sculptural see-through showers, platform tubs, sleek updates of traditional pedestal sinks, and walls of glass that open to the outdoors.

The style selected often reflects the decor of the rest of the home, though there is no rule of thumb that says French provincial or English country homes must have similarly styled bathrooms. In fact, it is often more exciting to introduce an element of surprise and create a potpourri of flavors. Today, many of the rooms in a home manifest a blend of traditions, and the bathroom is no exception. For instance, an old claw-foot placed in the center of a highly modern space can have a dynamic impact.

One important criterion to heed, though, is that there be some uniformity in scale, color, pattern, or texture when selecting fixtures, fittings, materials, and accessories. Such elements can provide a powerful sense of continuity regardless of whether the bathroom adheres to a specific style or boasts an eclectic mix.

Practical considerations must also be taken into account. Area rugs, comfortable upholstered chairs, fine wall coverings, and billowy curtains can create traditional romance, but owners should beware that water and humidity may not be kind to certain materials.

Opposite: THE MOORISH-STYLE ARCH IN THIS LARGE SUBURBAN BATHROOM INSPIRED THE ROOM'S ROMANTIC CASBAH FEELING. THE EFFECT WAS COMPLETED WITH A MIX OF SOLID AND PATTERNED GREEN-AND-WHITE TILES REMINISCENT OF THOSE POPULAR IN SPANISH-INFLUENCED NORTH AFRICAN DESIGN. DESERT-COLORED TILES PAVE THE FLOOR, SOFTENED IN FRONT OF THE TUB BY A SMALL ORIENTAL RUG. **Above:** THE SPARENESS OF AMISH CABINETRY WAS THE INSPIRATION FOR THIS BATHROOM'S DESIGN, WHICH ALSO HAS HINTS OF SCANDINAVIAN SIMPLICITY IN ITS STREAMLINED PEDESTAL SINK, PALE WOOD DADO, AND WHITE UPPER WALLS. BEIGE TILES FORMING A SUBTLE HONEYCOMB PATTERN ON THE FLOOR MAINTAIN THE NEUTRAL PALETTE, AS DOES THE WALNUT STORAGE UNIT. ASIDE FROM HOUSING TOWELS AND LINENS, THIS FREESTANDING UNIT CREATES A BARRIER THAT ENSURES PRIVACY FOR THE MORE PERSONAL AREA OF THE BATHROOM.

Above: MARIE ANTOINETTE WOULD HAVE LOVED THIS CAST-IRON TUB WITH ITS MATTE BLACK EXTERIOR AND GOLD-PLATED FEET. THE DECIDEDLY FRENCH MOOD IS INTENSIFIED BY A MARBLE FIREPLACE, AN ANTIQUE ARMOIRE (WHICH CONCEALS ENTERTAINMENT EQUIPMENT), AND WALLPAPER DISPLAYING A DELICATE, AIRY DESIGN. THE GLEAMING WOOD FLOOR IS GRACED BY TWO SMALL TILED SECTIONS, WHICH PROVIDE WATERPROOF SURFACES AND RESEMBLE AREA RUGS. **Opposite:** DECKED OUT IN A FRENCH STYLE THAT BEARS A FARMHOUSE-CUM-GARDEN FEELING, THIS BATHROOM INCLUDES A TUB WITH AN UNUSUAL LATTICE SURROUND. A PALE YELLOW-AND-BLUE FLORAL PRINT THAT ADDS TO THE PROVINCIAL TONE IS USED FOR THE SINK SKIRT, THE BALLOON SHADES, THE HAMPER LINING, AND EVEN THE TRIM OF THE UPHOLSTERED CHAIR. TO HEIGHTEN THE PASTORAL AMBIENCE, THE WALLS ARE COATED IN A PALE SHADE OF ROBIN'S-EGG BLUE.

Left: ASIDE FROM ITS OLD-FASHIONED-STYLE SINK, THIS BATHROOM COULD EASILY PASS AS AN ART-FILLED ENGLISH STUDY. A SMALL READING STAND SHOWCASES CURRENT PERIODICALS, WHILE A TABLE WITH AN ORNATE GILDED PEDESTAL DISPLAYS FAVORITE BOXES AND FRESH FLOWERS. IMPOSING GLASS CANDLESTICKS STAND TALL ON EITHER SIDE OF THE SINK AND, TOGETHER WITH AN ASSORTMENT OF DELICATE VIALS FILLED WITH COLORFUL LIQUIDS, CREATE THE IMAGE OF A SHRINE. STAINED GLASS, WHICH PICKS UP THE COLORS OF THE FLOOR TILES ARRANGED IN AN ELABORATE NEAR EASTERN DESIGN, FURTHER CONTRIBUTES TO THE ALMOST SPIRITUAL AMBIENCE.

Above: BATHED IN PALE BLUE AND ACCENTED WITH WHITE TRIM, THIS EXQUISITE BATHROOM LOOKS LIKE A PACKAGE FROM TIFFANY. THE CLAW-FOOT TUB, EMBRACED BY A STATELY ARCH, WAS PAINTED TO MATCH THE WALLS, WHICH CREATE A SUBDUED BACKDROP FOR THE ASSORTMENT OF COLLECTIBLES. THE LAVATORY IS HOUSED IN AN OLD BAR; A WICKER AND BAMBOO CHAIR IS PAIRED WITH AN ANTIQUE DRESSING TABLE; AND WALL-TO-WALL CARPETING IS ACCENTED WITH A SMALL NEEDLEPOINT RUG.

Below: Although the decor of this bathroom off a guest room seems somewhat spare, the amenities give visitors much more than a cold morning cleansing. A feeling of rejuvenation pervades the space, thanks to a new incarnation of a Victorian tub. Combined with a contemporary-style overscale mirror, crisp white wainscoting, and bare double-hung windows, the piece imbues the room with a fresh look.

Opposite: The owners of a large home could not resist turning an extra bedroom into a luxurious master bathroom, complete with a claw-foot tub displayed proudly between two grand windows that act as a frame. Other creature comforts include a sumptuous armchair, fully stocked built-in shelves, and a glorious view of an English wildflower garden. A weathered antique mirror, flanked by light fixtures of the same era, blends in readily with the old-fashioned tub to create a traditional tone.

Above: A tiny courtyard off this master bathroom provides a wonderful garden view from the traditional cast-iron tub. Sheer shades are rarely pulled down, except when the sun is too strong or when the bather wishes to block views.

Opposite: THE ECLECTIC BLEND IN THIS CHARMING BATHROOM HAS AN OVERALL TRADITIONAL TONE, THANKS TO THE EXTENSIVE USE OF DARK WOOD, WHICH ENGULFS THE TUB, FRAMES THE MIRROR, AND COVERS THE FLOOR. BUT A TRADITIONAL TONE DOES NOT HAVE TO SEEM ORDINARY, AS EVIDENCED BY THE NOVEL TOUCHES THAT ABOUND IN THE SPACE. SQUARE CUTOUTS FORM AN ORIGINAL, EYE-CATCHING FRINGE ON THE VALANCE, WHILE DIFFERENT FABRIC BEARING A SIMILAR LOOK DRESSES UP AN OLD PEDESTAL SINK. A COLLECTION OF POTTERY THAT ONE WOULD EXPECT TO SEE IN A LIVING ROOM RESTS ON THE BROAD LEDGE OF THE TUB, RESIDING SIDE-BY-SIDE WITH BOTTLES OF BATH OILS—THE MORE COMMON BATHROOM INHABITANTS. **Above:** HERE, A SITTING ROOM OFF A MASTER BEDROOM WAS TRANSFORMED INTO AN ENTICING BATHROOM. WITH ITS HARDWOOD FLOOR, HOOKED RUGS, PAINTED WOODEN MOLDING, ANTIQUE WOODEN CHAIR, AND STAINED GLASS WALL HANGINGS, THE SPACE RETAINS ITS SITTING-ROOM CHARACTER, MAKING IT A RELAXING SPOT FOR A BATH.

Above, left: PAINT WAS USED TO FRESHEN UP THIS SIMPLE BATHROOM IN A COST-EFFECTIVE WAY. WALLS AND WOODWORK WERE PAINTED A CLEAN, CRISP WHITE, AND A FLORAL DESIGN IN COUNTRY TONES WAS STENCILED NEAR THE CEILING, CREATING AN EFFECTIVE SUBSTITUTE FOR MOLDING. A SIMILAR PATTERN WAS STENCILED AROUND THE PERIMETER OF THE DARK GREEN PAINTED FLOOR, WHICH PREVENTS THE PREDOMINANTLY WHITE ROOM FROM APPEARING WASHED OUT. ALSO BREAKING UP THE VISUAL MONOTONY IS A SIMPLE BLACK VASE POSITIONED ON THE DECK OF THE TUB. **Above, right:** TO WARM UP THIS BATHROOM— BOTH PHYSICALLY AND AESTHETICALLY—A COLORFUL ORIENTAL RUG WAS PLACED OVER THE CERAMIC TILE FLOOR. THE RUG'S DEEP RED HUES AND SOFT TEXTURE COMBINE WITH THE RICH WOODS OF THE CABINETS AND PANELING TO MAKE THE LARGE SPACE SEEM MORE COZY AND INTIMATE. BLACK AND BEIGE TILES RUN AROUND THE PERIMETER OF THE FLOOR, CREATING A HANDSOME BORDER FOR THE RUG. SOOTHING BLUE-GRAY TRIM ACCENTS THE SHOWER STALL, WHICH INCLUDES A BENCH AND MIRROR. **Opposite:** TO GIVE THIS BATHROOM THE REFRESHING LOOK OF A SPRING DAY, THE UPPER PORTION OF THE WALLS WAS PAPERED WITH AN AIRY BLUE-AND-CREAM PATTERN. THE DADO, HOWEVER, WAS PAINTED SOLID WHITE IN ORDER TO PROVIDE A VISUAL BREAK BETWEEN THE DISTINCT DESIGNS OF THE WALLPAPER AND TILED FLOOR. A SIMPLE TRELLIS-PATTERNED SHOWER CURTAIN AND MATCHING VALANCE OFFER FURTHER IMAGES OF SPRING WITH THEIR FLORAL DESIGNS—YOU CAN PRACTICALLY SMELL THE DELICATE BLOOMS.

Opposite: CREATING AN AMBIENCE OF TRANQUILITY, THIS MODERN VERSION OF A JAPANESE SOAKING TUB TRANSPORTS THE BATHER TO THE ORIENT. A SHOJI SCREEN OPENS TO REVEAL THE SOOTHING GREENERY OF AN OUTDOOR GARDEN AND CLOSES TO MAINTAIN PRIVACY. **Right:** WITH A REFRESHINGLY SIMPLE DESIGN, THIS BATHROOM DEMONSTRATES HOW NATURE CAN BE BROUGHT INDOORS, EVEN INTO A UTILITARIAN SPACE. AN UNOBSTRUCTED WALL OF GLASS MAKES IT SEEM AS THOUGH THE PEACEFUL GARDEN BEYOND IS ACTUALLY PART OF THE BATHROOM. TWO FACING MIRRORS MULTIPLY THE IMAGE, THEREBY EXTENDING THE SERENITY AND MAKING THE NARROW SPACE SEEM EXPONENTIALLY LARGER. A SLATE FLOOR ADDS TO THE OUTDOOR SENSATION.

Opposite: WHEN A LOVER OF CONTEMPORARY ART ASKED THAT HER BATHROOM REFLECT THAT APPRECIATION, THE ARCHITECT MET THE CHALLENGE IN SEVERAL WAYS. THE DOOR LEADING INTO THE ROOM WAS DESIGNED WITH A GRID REMINISCENT OF A PIET MONDRIAN PAINTING, AND A THREE-DIMENSIONAL SCULPTURE OF CHUNKY FREE-FORM TRIANGLES WAS POSITIONED TO SERVE AS A SHOWER CURTAIN. THE REST OF THE ROOM WAS DELIBERATELY LEFT SPARE TO ALLOW THE "ART" TO STAND OUT.

Above: CONTEMPORARY IS SOMETIMES RELATIVE, AS IN THIS EARLY RANCH HOUSE, WHICH WAS CONSIDERED QUITE MODERN AT THE TIME IT WAS BUILT YET BECAME RATHER DATED OVER THE YEARS. THE NEW OWNERS KEPT THE ORIGINAL FIXTURES, BUT FRESHENED THE ROOM WITH A NEW COAT OF YELLOW PAINT IN A FAUX LEATHER FINISH THAT ECHOES THE WOOD DRAWERS AND TRIM. FURTHER ADDITIONS INCLUDE A NARROW WHITE WINDOW SHADE AND A PAIR OF MASSIVE ROUND MIRRORS.

Above: Multiple levels seem apropos in a bathroom that manifests a celestial theme with the help of a giant circular light fixture adorned by tiny stars. The same travertine is used on the floors, walls, and tub surround in order to maintain a sense of continuity between the different levels. Black accents in the form of border tiles, decorative columns, molding, and the inside of the whirlpool tub add drama suitable for an interplanetary voyage.

Right: GLASS BRICKS HAVE ENJOYED A REVIVAL BECAUSE OF THEIR ABILITY TO PROVIDE PRIVACY WHILE LETTING IN LIGHT. HERE, THEY GRACEFULLY CAMOUFLAGE THE TOILET CUBICLE, DEFTLY SECTIONING IT OFF FROM THE REST OF THE SPACE. AMPLE WHITE STORAGE TOPPED BY A SLEEK BLACK MARBLE COUNTERTOP ALLOWS THE SPACIOUS RETREAT TO SERVE AS A DRESSING ROOM AND FREES UP DRAWER SPACE IN THE BEDROOM. RECESSED LIGHTING TAKES THE PLACE OF OBTRUSIVE FIXTURES, THEREBY ADDING TO THE SMOOTH LOOK OF THE CONTEMPORARY SPACE.

Left: THE PORTHOLE-SHAPED LIGHTS AND THE WOODEN CABINETRY AND TRIM WERE INSPIRED BY A LOVE OF BOATS. THE WOOD IS COMPLEMENTED BY A MARBLE COUNTERTOP AND TILE FLOOR THAT ADD SIMILAR BUT DISTINCT EARTHY SHADES. A GLASS BRICK WALL SEEN THROUGH THE MIRROR ADDS DIMENSION AND SCREENS THE BATHING AREA. **Below:** ON THE TOP LEVEL OF A SECLUDED MODERN BEACH HOUSE, A LARGE SHOWER IS JUST BARELY SCREENED BY TWO SHORT WALLS OF FROSTED GLASS THAT SERVE PRIMARILY TO RESTRICT THE SPRAY OF WATER. AN IMMENSE PICTURE WINDOW PROVIDES A GLORIOUS VIEW OF THE OCEAN WHILE CLEANSING.

Opposite: WHILE THE SHAPE AND FITTINGS OF THIS TUB ARE TRADITIONAL, ITS STAINLESS STEEL FEET AND CENTRAL PLACEMENT IN THE BATHROOM LEAVE NO DOUBT THAT THE SPACE BELONGS TO SOMEONE WITH A SENSE OF DARING. A LONG, NARROW MIRROR THAT APPEARS TO REST PRECARIOUSLY ON A SMALL LEDGE ADDS TO THE FEELING OF RISK, EVEN THOUGH THE MIRROR IS ACTUALLY FIRMLY ANCHORED. BUILT-IN STORAGE, DEVOID OF ANY DISTRACTING HARDWARE, LINES THE WINDOW WALL.

Adding Color

The color or combination of colors selected for a bathroom is as important in creating a mood as are the style and period of the fixtures and accessories. Among the key decisions is whether to go with a monochromatic or mixed palette. The next step is to decide what type of color or colors to use.

Manufacturers of bathroom-related items have developed so many colorful lines that zeroing in can sometimes prove difficult. Many of these elements, such as paints, wallpaper, towels, and accessories, are relatively inexpensive and can easily be changed.

One of the all-time favorite monochromatic options is the all-white bathroom. Beware, however, that even within the white category there are subtle variations, which run from a crisp milk color to a buttery tone. Mixing different whites together requires a deft hand to ensure that the combination looks like a deliberate choice

rather than an unfortunate mistake.

There are also monochromatic palettes that appeal to homeowners who want a bit more color. Some favor green in order to bring in the outdoors, some black to impart a sense of drama, and some gray or beige to inject sophistication.

For still others, bathrooms are the best places to let loose and have some decorating fun by mixing many different colors that may be considered too provocative to showcase elsewhere in the home, particularly in the more public spaces. In many cases, children's bathrooms are the best laboratories in which to experiment with a riot of colors, because kids remain the least inhibited guinea pigs when it comes to mixing and matching.

Opposite: CREATING THE SENSATION OF BEING IN A FISH TANK, THIS COLORFUL BATHROOM IS DECKED OUT IN SHADES OF AQUA AND ROYAL BLUE, WHICH APPEAR IN THE MIX OF GEOMETRIC TILES AS WELL AS ON THE PAINTED CABINETRY. A FEW ROWS OF YELLOW SUGGEST SAND OR SUN, DEPENDING ON ONE'S IMAGINATION. BLUE TOWELS AND A BLUE MIRROR FRAME FURTHER CONTRIBUTE TO THE UNDERWATER AMBIENCE. **Above:** BY ANGLING THE SHOWER AND SLANTING THE EDGES OF THE VANITY, THE OWNERS OF THIS ALL-WHITE MASTER BATHROOM WERE ABLE TO FIT ALL THE ACCOUTREMENTS THEY WANTED INTO THE NARROW SPACE. THE USE OF WHITE ON EVERYTHING FROM THE FLOOR TO THE CEILING ENLARGES THE ROOM VISUALLY, AS DO THE ALL-GLASS SHOWER STALL AND THE LARGE MIRROR ABOVE THE VANITY. ACCENTS OF BLACK ALONG THE EDGE OF THE VANITY AND AROUND THE RIM OF THE BASIN ADD DIMENSION.

Above: AN OLD-FASHIONED TUB WITH GOLD-PLATED FEET WAS PLACED ADJACENT TO A CURVING WALL OF WINDOWS THAT LOOKS OUT ONTO A PORCH AND THE WOODS BEYOND, OFFERING PLEASANT VISTAS. HINTS OF ROSE IN THE MOSTLY WHITE FLOOR TILES ARE PICKED UP BY THE OVERHEAD LIGHT FIXTURE AND THE FLOWERS.

Below: WORN WOOD PLANKING, PALE YELLOW PAINT ON THE UPPER PORTION OF THE WALLS, AND SOME STAINLESS STEEL TOUCHES HELP TO SOFTEN AN OTHERWISE VERY WHITE BATHROOM. DELICATE WHITE SHEERS BUNCHED TOGETHER AT THE WINDOW AND A SMALL BATH MAT ADD SOME TEXTURE AND CONTRAST TO THE OTHERWISE SMOOTH SURFACES OF THE ROOM.

Above: WHITE COMES IN VARIATIONS THAT RANGE FROM QUIET TO OBVIOUS, AND HERE THE GAMUT ADDS A RICHNESS THAT GIVES THE ROOM ITS REFINED YET LIVED-IN LOOK. IN THE CATEGORY OF ULTRAWHITE ARE THE PORCELAIN TUB, MARBLE FLOOR, SEMISHEER CURTAINS, PAINTED WALLS, AND CABINETS. MEANWHILE, THE UPHOLSTERED CHAIR SEAT, A BATHSIDE TABLE FOR RESTING A GLASS OF WATER OR A BOOK, A TERRY CLOTH ROBE, AND A TOWEL CASUALLY DRAPED OVER THE EDGE OF THE TUB INTRODUCE A SLIGHT CREAM SHADE. THE ONLY TRULY NONWHITE ELEMENTS ARE THE WOODEN MIRROR FRAME AND THE SUBTLE GRAY VEINING OF THE MARBLE COUNTERTOP.

Opposite: THE OWNER OF THIS BATHROOM/DRESSING SUITE PROUDLY DEBUNKED THE DECORATING ADAGE OF NOT USING TOO MUCH COLOR OR PATTERN IN A SMALL ROOM. AS A RESULT, THE ROOM EXUDES A SENSE OF EXUBERANCE WITH ITS LIVELY RED-AND-WHITE PATTERNED WALLPAPER AND COORDINATING SINK SKIRT AND SEAT CUSHION. THESE PROVINCIAL-LOOKING FABRICS PROVIDE A WELCOME SOFT COUNTERPOINT TO THE RICH POMPEIAN-RED TEXTURED DESIGN OF THE DADO AND THE DEEP HUE OF THE CARPET. HORSE PRINTS REFLECT A FAVORITE PASSION OF THE WOMAN WHO USES THE ROOM. **Above, left:** HERE, THE MOOD IS CLEARLY TRADITIONAL, THANKS TO THE OLD-FASHIONED PEDESTAL SINK WITH GOLD-PLATED FITTINGS, THE ANTIQUE MIRROR, THE COLLECTION OF ARTWORK AND CERAMICS, AND THE FAUX TORTOISESHELL FINISH OF THE UPPER WALLS. BUT IT WAS A LOVE OF COLOR THAT INSPIRED THE DEEP TURQUOISE HUE OF THE WAINSCOTING AND THE TUB ENCLOSURE. A CRANBERRY-COLORED TOWEL ADDS A SPARK OF FESTIVITY. **Above, right:** SELECTING A COLOR THAT WOULD MAINTAIN THE RICHNESS AND DEPTH OF THE MAHOGANY CABINETRY, THE BLACK MARBLE COUNTERTOP, AND THE TUB SURROUND WAS A DIFFICULT TASK. THE OWNER OF THIS SMALL BATHROOM SETTLED ON A RUSTY HUE, WITH A MATTE FINISH FOR THE DADO AND A FAUX MARBLE FINISH BEARING TOUCHES OF ROSE FOR THE UPPER WALLS. VENETIAN BLINDS ADD A TRADITIONAL TOUCH AT THE WINDOW.

Below: TRANSFORMING THIS BATHROOM INTO A PIECE OF ABSTRACT ART, THE DESIGNER STAINED THE CABINETS AND DRAWERS OF THE VANITY WITH DIFFERENT SHADES OF RED, GREEN, AND OCHER, WHICH ADD UNUSUAL ZIP TO THE SPACE. THE WOOD FLOORING WAS STAINED A DARK COLOR, SERVING AS A VISUAL ANCHOR, AND TWO LARGE MIRRORS WERE FRAMED IN PALE MAPLE FOR CONTRAST. THE COUNTERTOP IS ONE LONG EXPANSE OF GRAY MARBLE THAT BLENDS WELL WITH THE OTHER COLORS. **Opposite:** HERE, BLACK IS USED EXTENSIVELY TO INJECT URBAN SOPHISTICATION INTO THE BATHROOM OF A HOME LOCATED IN THE MIDDLE OF A RUGGED CANYON. THIS SENSE OF CONTRAST IS CARRIED OUT FURTHER BY PITTING THE BLACK TILES AND COUNTER-TOP AGAINST PALE WOOD CABINETRY. THE WINDOWS, WITH THEIR METAL GRID, HEIGHTEN THE URBAN SENSATION, DESPITE THE FACT THAT THEY OVER-LOOK A NONURBAN LANDSCAPE.

Above: COLOR CAN BE SUBTLE, AS EVIDENCED BY THIS GRAY AND PALE WOOD BATHROOM. GRAY MARBLE LINES THE FLOOR, THE TUB ENCLOSURE, AND THE WALLS TO CREATE A CALMING FEELING, WHILE A LONG, NARROW NICHE STORES GRAY-AND-WHITE STRIPED TOWELS THAT PROVIDE VIVID CONTRAST. GOLD DETAILING FOR THE SHOWER ROD, DOOR HANDLE, AND TILE INSETS ADDS A BIT OF GLITZ.

Right: WHITE AND BLACK CREATE A TIMELESS COMBINATION IN THIS BATHROOM THAT HAS A BIT OF AN ART DECO FLAIR. BLACK MARBLE ON THE FLOOR ANCHORS THE LARGE SPACE AND IS REPEATED ON THE COUNTERTOP. A CHECKER-BOARD PATTERN RIMS THE CURVED SHOWER FLOOR WHILE A NARROW LINE OF DIAMONDS ZIPS ALONG THE SHOWER WALL, BENEATH THE WINDOW, AND AROUND THE WHIRLPOOL TUB, ADDING A BIT OF ZEST TO THE SPACE.

Above: A LOVE OF MODERN ART INSPIRED THE USE OF ABSTRACT PAINTED TILES ALONG THE FLOOR AND ON ONE WALL OF A GLASS-DOORED SHOWER. THE EFFECT IS SUGGESTIVE OF A JACKSON POLLACK PAINTING. BY COVERING THE OTHER WALLS WITH PLAIN GRAY TILES AND SELECTING A SIM-PLE PEDESTAL SINK, THE OWNERS PREVENTED THE SPACE FROM BECOMING TOO OVERWHELMING.

Above: IN THIS PRETEEN'S BATHROOM, A COLORFUL FISH MOTIF IS REPEATED ON THE SHOWER CURTAIN AND ON THE WALLPAPER BORDER AT THE TOP OF THE STALL. THE TRIM AROUND THE SHOWER IS PAINTED A GLORIOUS BLUE-GREEN REMINISCENT OF CARIBBEAN WATERS, AND THE ARRAY OF TOWELS BRINGS TOGETHER ALL THE DIFFERENT COLORS OF THE WALLPAPER, SHOWER CURTAIN, AND RAG RUG.

Below: THIS SWEET BATHROOM, DESIGNED FOR TWO YOUNG BUDDING BALLERINAS, HAS GREAT STAYING POWER AND WILL CONTINUE TO BE APPROPRIATE YEARS FROM NOW WHEN THE GIRLS ARE OLDER AND THEIR INTERESTS HAVE CHANGED. THE GRAY-AND-WHITE CHECKERBOARD FLOOR IS QUITE GROWN-UP, AS IS THE DIAGONALLY STRIPED MAROON WALLPAPER. THE ONLY NECESSARY MODIFICATIONS WILL BE A NEW SET OF TOWELS AND A MORE APPROPRIATE CHAIR.

Above: MANY MANUFACTURERS OFFER SINKS IN THE CRAYON COLORS KIDS LOVE. HERE, BRIGHT RED LIVENS UP A TRADITIONAL SINK, AS DO MIS-MATCHED FAUCET HANDLES. TO ADD ADDITIONAL PIZZAZZ, THE FLOOR WAS LAID IN TILES THAT FORM A CRAZY PATCHWORK QUILT WITH THEIR ZANY MIX OF COLORS AND PATTERNS. THE BOLD MÉLANGE IS SURE TO DELIGHT YOUNG USERS, AS WELL AS THEIR PARENTS, WHO WILL APPRECIATE ITS DIRT-HIDING CAPABILITY.

Spalike Retreats

When space is no object and the budget is generous, there is no limit to the options available today for decorating or remodeling a bathroom. Many overscale bathrooms are referred to as spas because these rooms promise the ultimate in comfort and sybaritic pleasure. Often they include amenities similar to those found at well-equipped health centers and gyms, thereby bringing the facilities and luxuries of the outside world into the home.

The more elaborate home spas include his-and-her toilet cubicles, double lavatories with generous storage, a tub raised on a platform or sunk into the floor, a walk-in shower with multiple water effects, exercise equipment, dressing areas, and sometimes even a sauna. If the space exists, some people transform these rooms into something closer to a living space with comfortable seating, entertainment equipment such as televisions and stereos, and even small refrigerators. The most envied examples boast the additional luxury of opening onto a deck or courtyard.

Part of the secret to many of these rooms is found in the details, not just the amenities, for they provide that individual design stamp known as panache. Such decorative devices might include gold-plated fittings for a very luxe look, an assortment of lush plants to create an indoor oasis, or dazzling accent tiles that add some glitz. Together, the right fixtures and details can have a stand-up-and-take-notice effect.

Opposite: Abutting French doors that open onto a deck overlooking the woods, this spalike tub with whirlpool jets provides its occupants with the feeling of bathing outdoors. Rimmed by the same rustic brick that is used for the home's garden paths, the tub further suggests an outdoor retreat. Plants grace the edge of the tub, reflecting the greenery of the home's surroundings. **Above:** Nestled between matching lavatories, a whirlpool tub conjures up the image of an ancient Roman spa with its luxurious marble surround and gold fittings. But this bathroom is no literal translation. Contemporary amenities include wall-to-wall carpeting, a large picture window left uncurtained, good artificial lighting, generous storage, and a rustic wood ceiling with decorative beams.

Above: TAKING ITS CUE FROM THE SURROUNDING RUGGED HILLS, THIS DRAMATIC SPA FEATURES A MIX OF EARTHY MATERIALS: MARBLE SPORTING DEEP TONES OF BROWN AND BLUE, BLUE-GRAY CONCRETE, AND FROSTED GLASS TILES. THE OVERSIZE TUB-CUM-SHOWER OFFERS A PANOPLY OF FAUCETS, STEAM FITTINGS, AND HANDHELD SPRAYS SO THAT BATHERS HAVE THEIR CHOICE OF WATER EFFECTS—AS FINE AS A MIST OR AS DRENCHING AS A JUNGLE RAIN. THE PEAKED ROOF, INSET WITH GLASS, USHERS IN STREAMS OF LIGHT. **Opposite:** "UNIQUE" IS THE WORD MOST USE WHEN THEY VIEW THIS COMPARTMENTALIZED BATHROOM, WHICH IS ENVELOPED IN A WARM MULTITONED BROWN MARBLE THAT UNIFIES THE SPACE. A CURVING GLASS-BLOCK WALL ACTS AS A SCREEN BETWEEN THE DRESSING AREA AND THE MORE ELEMENTARY COMPONENTS OF THE BATHROOM, WHILE A SIMILAR BARRIER SEPARATES THE SHOWER AND TOILET. SWINGING DOORS REMINISCENT OF THOSE FOUND IN OLD SALOONS GIVE THE SPACE A WESTERN FEELING.

Below: TUCKED INTO A LARGE CORNER, A WHIRLPOOL TUB WAS RAISED OFF THE GROUND SO THAT THE BATHER COULD BEST ENJOY THE VIEW PROVIDED BY AN EXPANSE OF TALL, UNCURTAINED WINDOWS. ADDITIONAL WINDOWS ABOVE BRING WELCOME LIGHT INTO THE HIGH-CEILINGED ROOM, WHICH, WITH ITS BLUE-AND-WHITE COLOR SCHEME, CREATES THE SENSATION OF BATHING IN THE SEA.

Above: THIS OVERSIZE WHIRLPOOL TUB IS THE INDOOR EQUIVALENT OF A HOT TUB. CAPABLE OF ACCOMMODATING SEVERAL USERS SIMULTANEOUSLY, IT IS SITUATED BENEATH A SLANTED CEILING IN A COZY ALCOVE JUST BEYOND THE CONVERSATION AREA OF A FAMILY ROOM. A SKYLIGHT BATHES THE ROOM IN SUNLIGHT, WHILE NATURAL WOOD FLOORING AND TRIM COMPLEMENT THE DESIGN.

Below: WITH THE HELP OF A FREESTANDING VANITY CRAFTED FROM HANDSOME TEAK, HIS-AND-HER BATHROOMS WERE CARVED OUT OF A SINGLE SPACE. A VAST MIRROR SET WITHIN A BOLD BLACK GRID THAT HAS A CONTEMPORARY ORIENTAL FLAVOR PROVIDES A MEASURE OF PRIVACY FOR EACH SIDE WHILE ALLOWING COMMUNICATION BETWEEN THE TWO AREAS. AN ALVAR AALTO CHAIR AND TABLE ALLOW THE OCCUPANTS TO KEEP EACH OTHER COMPANY COMFORTABLY. OVERHEAD, A CIRCULAR SKYLIGHT BRINGS IN NATURAL LIGHT.

Above: THIS SPACIOUS BATHROOM, WHICH IS THE SIZE OF MANY BEDROOMS, FEATURES DISTINCT AREAS FOR BATHING, SHOWERING, AND PRIMPING. A TELEVISION MOUNTED OVERHEAD PERMITS USERS TO CATCH THE NEWS OR A FAVORITE SHOW, AND A HIGHLY EFFICIENT YET MINIMALIST-LOOKING STAND PROVIDES A RESTING PLACE FOR THE REMOTE CONTROL, AS WELL AS TOWELS AND A TELEPHONE. THE MOOD IS COOL AND SLEEK BECAUSE OF THE PRIMARILY BLACK-AND-WHITE COLOR SCHEME.

Opposite: CONCEIVED AS A TRUE BATHROOM GETAWAY, THIS ROOM IS LIGHT YEARS AHEAD OF MOST IN ITS AVANT-GARDE DESIGN. THE TWO LAVATORIES PRESENT A VISUALLY EXCITING JUXTAPOSITION, WITH THE BASIN OF ONE JUTTING OUT FROM THE WALL AND THE BASIN OF THE OTHER SUBMERGED IN A GLASS-TOP TABLE. A TUB SUNK INTO THE SLATE FLOOR INVITES WEARY BODIES TO COLLAPSE RIGHT INTO ITS SOOTHING WATERS, AND A NEARBY HEATED TOWEL RACK MAKES EMERGING EASIER WHEN THE REAL WORLD CALLS. AN OVERSIZE CHAIN AND PADLOCK SUGGEST A LONGING TO BE KEPT PRISONER IN THIS PLEASURABLE RETREAT. **Above:** ALTHOUGH THIS LUXURIOUS BATHROOM FOR TWO APPEARS TO DEMONSTRATE PERFECT SYMMETRY AT FIRST GLANCE, THERE ARE ACTUALLY SUBTLE DIFFERENCES IN THE CONFIGURATIONS OF THE STORAGE UNITS DUE TO THE DISTINCT NEEDS OF EACH PARTY. OTHER ELEMENTS OF SURPRISE ARE THE ELEVATED GLASS COUNTERTOPS, WHICH PROVIDE FULL VIEWS OF THE BASINS, MAKING THEM APPEAR AS GIANT GLASS BOWLS RESTING ATOP THE CABINETS AND DRAWERS. RECESSED LIGHTING MAINTAINS THE AREA'S SLEEK LOOK, WHICH HAS BEEN ACHIEVED THROUGH AN ABUNDANT USE OF GLASS.

Below: JUST THE RIGHT AMOUNT OF WOOD WAS USED IN THIS TWO-PERSON MASTER BATHROOM TO CREATE A SENSE OF WARMTH AND PERMANENCE WITHOUT MAKING THE SPACE SEEM TOO DARK OR FOREBODING. THE DARK WOOD CASINGS, BEAMS, AND CABINETRY ARE COUNTERBALANCED BY THE SOFT GRAY MARBLE USED FOR THE SINK COUNTERTOP, BACKSPLASH, TUB SURROUND, AND BUILT-IN SHELVES. A MIRRORED WALL AND BARE WINDOWS OPEN UP THE SPACE, PREVENTING IT FROM SEEMING CRAMPED WHEN BOTH PARTIES ARE PRESENT.

Above: INSTEAD OF BEING USED FOR PLANTS, A GREENHOUSE WAS RETROFITTED TO ACCOMMODATE A LARGE WHIRLPOOL. THE LOOK IS CRISP, WITH A WHITE TUB, WHITE CERAMIC TILES, AND WHITE LINEN SHADES. THE CHAIR ADDS A BIT OF WHIMSY WITH ITS PAINTED FACE AND WINGS.

Opposite: SOME OWNERS PREFER THEIR WHIRLPOOLS TO BE PART OF THEIR BEDROOMS. HERE, AN INDOOR GARDEN OASIS HAS BEEN CREATED AROUND THE BATHING AREA, WHILE THE SLEEPING AREA (REFLECTED IN THE MIRROR) IS SHROUDED IN RUSTIC WOOD, APPEARING IN THE FORM OF PANELING, MULLIONS, AND FURNITURE. WOODEN CEILING BEAMS BRING THE TWO AREAS TOGETHER, WHILE A SKYLIGHT AND PLENTY OF WINDOWS KEEP THE ENTIRE SPACE LIGHT AND AIRY.

Above: THIS MASTER BATHROOM TAKES MAXIMUM ADVANTAGE OF THE HOME'S LUSHLY LANDSCAPED PROPERTY. THE WHIRLPOOL TUB AND GLASS-DOORED SHOWER ARE SITUATED IN FRONT OF A GIANT PANE OF GLASS THAT LOOKS OUT ONTO A WELL-SCREENED COURTYARD. THE EARTHY TONES OF BOTH THE VANITY AND THE METALLIC COPPER TILES SPECKLING THE FLOOR, WALLS, TUB, AND SHOWER COMPLEMENT THE OUTDOOR VIEW.

Below: DEVOID OF ANY CURTAINS OR SOLID PARTITIONS, THE SHOWER AND TUB IN THIS RELATIVELY NARROW SPA ARE SEPARATED BY ONLY A SINGLE STEP. AN ASSORTMENT OF TERRA-COTTA TILES ENVELOPS THE SPACE, WHICH EXUDES A DEFINITE FAR EASTERN TONE. THE DIFFERENT SHAPES AND SIZES OF THE TILES ADD VARIETY AND TEXTURE TO THE MONOCHROMATIC SPACE.

Above: THIS BATHROOM MAY BE SMALL, BUT ITS PLEASURES ARE DOUBLED BY AN ADJACENT DECK. AFTER SOAKING UP SOME SUN, USERS CAN RETREAT TO THE INDOORS AND SHOWER OR BATHE AMID A WHITE TILED OASIS TRIMMED IN NATURAL WOOD THAT ECHOES THE DECK.

Part Two

Kitchens

INTRODUCTION

"No matter where I serve my guests, they seem to like my kitchen best." This popular saying, which for years has graced items as random as refrigerator magnets and needlepoint hangings, has withstood the test of time and turned into somewhat of a self-fulfilling prophecy. For today the kitchen is undoubtedly the most popular, and possibly the most important, room in the home.

Proof of the kitchen's popularity has been well documented. An official of the National Home Builders Association recently declared that a home won't sell unless it has a kitchen of excellent quality, with plenty of space and state-of-the-art appliances. That statement, in tandem with the fact that in the past twenty-five years the average size of a home has increased by six hundred square feet (54sq.m), means that certain rooms in the home—most notably, kitchens—have been designed larger. This increase in size is a direct response to an increase in the room's functionality.

Historically, kitchens existed only for the preparation of meals. In medieval England it was common to find the kitchen completely removed from the home, as a separate structure, thus containing all the smells and messes associated with that room. It wasn't until the sixteenth century that the cooking and living areas came to be housed under one roof, albeit with separate entrances. These kitchens, however, were often dimly lit and poorly ventilated, especially in the case of those found below the main level of a home. However, the kitchen as we know it primarily evolved in the eighteenth and nineteenth centuries when the range and precursors to the appliances we take for granted today, like refrigerators and dishwashers, were developed.

Some of the most progressive changes in the idea of the kitchen have occurred in the twentieth century. Kitchen design changed as a result of the changing role of women in society. Traditionally, kitchens were intended

Opposite: IN TRADITIONAL EUROPEAN KITCHENS, PLATE RACKS LIKE THE ONES SHOWN HERE WERE NORMALLY FOUND ABOVE A SINK WHERE THEY PROVIDED A CONVENIENT PLACE TO STORE AND DRY DISHES. IN CONTEMPORARY NORTH AMERICAN KITCHENS, HOWEVER, PLATE RACKS ARE ALSO DECORATIVE, DISPLAYING AS WELL AS STORING ATTRACTIVE DISHES.

for a sole cook, more commonly known as the housewife. As women moved out of the home and into the workplace, kitchens were slowly but surely redesigned and rescaled to accommodate more than one person preparing and cooking meals, or just grabbing a quick snack.

Above: THIS ROOM IS ALL ABOUT WOOD PLANKS, VARYING IN SIZE FROM BEADBOARD THIN TO LARGER SLATS FOR DRAWER COVERS. STANDING IN STARK CONTRAST TO ALL THE HORIZONTAL IMAGES IS A VERTICAL COLUMN THAT SEPARATES KITCHEN FROM DINING AREA. BLUE AND GREEN ACCENT THE WARM WOOD TONES OF THE ROOM, FROM THE WINDOW SEAT CUSHIONS TO THE STOOLS, AND EVEN ON THE WINDSOR CHAIRS THAT FLANK THE DINING TABLE.

Having more people working in the kitchen invariably led to more people lounging in the kitchen, and so the room evolved from a strictly utilitarian place to one that is more multipurpose and even surprisingly comfortable. Traditional boundaries were shattered and kitchens came to encompass the dining room and sometimes even the living room in a combination that was dubbed the "great room." Faster than you could say "a star is born," the kitchen became the center of family life.

That's an honor not likely to change anytime soon. For as quickly as the role of the kitchen has changed, manufacturers are just a step ahead with appliances to make working in this room so much easier, it will soon be almost a no-brainer. For example, at the time of this writing, at least one major manufacturer is developing voice-activated appliances, including ovens, microwaves, refrigerators and even washer/dryers. Electronics manufacturers have also embraced the kitchen, expanding and marketing their lines to include items like kitchen-sized televisions with built-in VCRs that mount or easily slide in under cabinets so one can watch TV or perhaps an instructional video while preparing a meal.

This is only a glimpse into what the future holds for the kitchen, and with the recent wave of technological advances, it seems that almost anything that can be imagined can be created.

Above: FABRIC CAN HIDE A MULTITUDE OF SINS, AS THIS SPACE DEMONSTRATES. BECAUSE THE LEFT AND RIGHT WALLS ARE SO HEAVY WITH CABINETRY, THE DESIGNER CHOSE TO HANG A GINGHAM CURTAIN FROM THE SINK COUNTER INSTEAD OF MOUNTING CABINETS UNDERNEATH. THE FABRIC ADDS SOFTNESS AND TEXTURE TO THE ROOM AND TIES IN WITH THE COLORS OF THE FLOOR AND WINDOW TREATMENT. IN ADDITION, FABRIC WAS USED TO LINE THE INSIDE OF THE UPPER CABINET DOORS TO HIDE CLUTTER STORED BEHIND THEM.

The New Country Kitchen

In the past, using the word "country" to describe a kitchen brought to mind very distinct images of handicraft, including do-it-yourself touches like frilly curtains, stenciled walls, weathered cabinets, and painted floors. Today, however, the country kitchen has grown up, and is no longer as much about adopting a stereotypical country style as it is about bringing the feeling of a weekend in the country indoors. Frilly curtains have been replaced by windows covered with shades or blinds, or nothing more than a wonderful view; stenciled walls are now dressed in tile; cabinets look aged, but not necessarily weathered; and floors are still painted, but with more sophisticated, geometric designs.

This new country kitchen retains qualities of the traditional, but is reinterpreted to look fresher by mixing in contemporary features. The most prominent of these features are professional quality or professional looking appliances, which have gained popularity in recent years. A large, stainless steel stove has become a staple in many kitchens, and as demonstrated on the following pages, can meld into almost any interior, thanks to well-thought-out interior design decisions, like choice of cabinetry and flooring materials.

Color also plays an important role, for there is no better way to bring the look and feel of the country indoors than with color. Bucolic shades of green, the warm red colors of autumn leaves, even pigments reminiscent of ponds, whether used on cabinets, painted floors or tiles, evoke the feeling of the outdoors. In a monochromatic kitchen, color is sometimes introduced in the form of collections displayed on open shelves or windowsills.

Perhaps the most obvious, and sometimes most challenging, way to bring the outdoors in, is to do it by literally using stone or brick for floors and logs of wood instead of planks for walls and ceilings. These are not always the most practical or affordable materials, but with a lot of determination (and perspiration) can be used to create a truly beautiful room.

Opposite: A RUSTIC FARM TABLE, WHICH DOES DOUBLE DUTY AS A SPACE FOR PREPARING MEALS—OR DEVOURING THEM— IS COMBINED WITH PIECES LIKE A PAIR OF WOODEN ROCKING CHAIRS AND RAG RUGS TO ADD A TOUCH OF COUNTRY WARMTH TO AN OTHERWISE STREAMLINED SPACE.

Left: THIS KITCHEN IN A 1960S HOLLYWOOD HILLS HOME WAS UPDATED TO THE PRESENT, WHILE RETAINING TRACES OF A "GROOVIER" ERA: COBALT-BLUE-PAINTED WINDOW FRAMES, TERRA-COTTA TILES FOR COUNTERTOP AND BACK-SPLASH, AND STIPPLED GREEN LINOLEUM FLOORS. THE CABINETS ARE SLAB WOOD PAINTED A FAUX GRAIN FINISH, WITH WROUGHT-IRON HARDWARE.

Opposite: THE SCULPTURALLY SHAPELY LEGS OF A SINK ADD A TOUCH OF WHIMSY TO A SMALL SPACE. BEADBOARD PANELING, USED HERE FOR BOTH WAINSCOTING AND CABINET LINING, IS TRADITIONALLY USED IN CONJUNCTION WITH MORE CASUAL MATERIALS, BUT WHEN PAINTED WHITE, WONDERFULLY COMPLEMENTS A MARBLE COUNTERTOP AND CONTEMPORARY FAUCET.

Right: A SPACIOUS, ALL-WHITE KITCHEN IS WARMED UP BY GREEN MARBLE FLOORING, SUNLIGHT STREAMING IN THROUGH A WALL OF WINDOWS THAT OVERLOOK A BAY, AND SOFT LIGHTS CLEVERLY RECESSED INTO A TRAY CEILING.

Above: A VICTORIAN-STYLE TABLE, MADE OF AN ORNATE WROUGHT-IRON BASE AND FUNCTIONAL BUTCHER BLOCK TOP, IS THE CENTERPIECE OF A KITCHEN THAT FEATURES WALL AND FLOOR TILES MORE COMMONLY FOUND IN BATHROOMS AND THE EVER-POPULAR PROFESSIONAL RANGE OVEN. COUNTRY ELEMENTS ABOUND, FROM GINGHAM VALANCES TO A COLLECTION OF ANIMAL PITCHERS ON THE WINDOWSILL OVER THE SINK.

Above: VIBRANT GREEN-PAINTED CABINETRY, PACKED WITH PLATES, MUGS, AND COLLECTIBLES, BOLDLY CONTRASTS A STARK WHITE TILE COUNTER AND ACCOMPANYING COOKTOP, BOTH MOUNTED ON INDUSTRIAL STEEL TUBING MORE COMMONLY FOUND IN RESTAURANT KITCHENS. HERE, ONE CAN EAT FROM ANTIQUE BLUE AND WHITE CHINA WHILE SITTING ON A MODERN CLASSIC, AN ALVAR AALTO STOOL.

Opposite: MISMATCHED WOODEN CHAIRS WITH COLORFUL CUSHIONS, A PAIR OF TABLE LAMPS PLACED ON A STAINLESS COUNTER, BAMBOO ROLLER SHADES AND A COLLECTION OF WOODEN ANIMALS ON THE WINDOWSILL ARE ALL TOUCHES THAT MAKE THIS A ROOM TO LINGER IN LONG AFTER A MEAL IS FINISHED. **Above:** A PAIR OF LONG PLATE RACKS ABOVE THE SINK SERVE TWO PURPOSES: TO FACILITATE DRYING, AS WELL AS STORING DISHES. HAND-FINISHED CABINETS BEAR AN INSCRIPTION OF ROMAN NUMERALS, PERHAPS COMMEMORATING THE YEAR THIS EUROPEAN COUNTRY-STYLE KITCHEN WAS COMPLETED.

Above: THE LOOK OF COUNTRY HAS ALWAYS BEEN ABOUT BRINGING THE COLORS OF NATURE INSIDE. HERE, CABINETS PAINTED ROBIN'S EGG BLUE WITH YELLOW ACCENT TRIM THAT MATCHES ADJACENT WALLS SET A LIVELY MOOD IN AN ENGLISH COUNTRY KITCHEN. **Opposite:** BRIGHT ORANGE MAY NOT BE THE FIRST COLOR ONE THINKS OF TO USE IN THE KITCHEN, BUT IT WORKS HERE. A WALL DECORATED IN ALTERNATING BRIGHT ORANGE AND STYLIZED FLORAL CERAMIC TILES PLAYS ON THE COLOR OF A FRENCH STOVE AND THE WARM TONE OF A HARDWOOD FLOOR. THE SOFT-TONED WOOD FURNITURE IN THE BREAKFAST NOOK REINFORCES THE EFFECT.

Above: A FLOOR PAINTED IN A COLOR TO MATCH CABINETS DISTRACTS THE EYE FROM THE CLUTTERED WALL AND COUNTER SPACES FILLED WITH KITCHEN TOOLS AND CURIOUS COLLECTIONS ON OPEN SHELVES. **Left:** A TWIG MOTIF USUALLY SIGNALS A MORE RUSTIC INTERIOR, BUT WHEN PAINTED A SHADE OF OFF-WHITE, IT TAKES ON A MORE SOPHISTICATED PERSONALITY AND ADDS TEXTURE TO THIS MONOCHROMATIC KITCHEN.

Below, left: IT'S ALL IN THE DETAILS.... A COLLECTION OF FRENCH APÉRITIF PITCHERS—INCLUDING TWO "SUZE" PITCHERS, WHICH PLAY OFF THE OWNER OF THIS KITCHEN'S NAME—SHARE SHELF SPACE WITH A MINIATURE MICHELIN MAN, A COLLECTION OF AMERICAN POTTERY, AND A STACK OF COLORFUL HAND TOWELS.

Below, right: A WALL MONTAGE OF MIX-AND-MATCH HAND-PAINTED CERAMIC TILES IS AN INTERESTING BACKDROP FOR A SLIGHTLY STAID BLACK CAST-IRON STOVE. THE SHELF BUILT IN ABOVE IT TAKES ON AN ARMOIRE-LIKE QUALITY DUE TO THE USE OF CURVED MOLDINGS, PAINTED GREEN TO COMPLEMENT THE TILES AND CABINETRY.

Above: TO BRIDGE THE STYLE GAP BETWEEN NEW, PROFESSIONAL APPLIANCES AND AGED CHERRY CABINETRY, THE DESIGNER OF THIS NEW ENGLAND FARMHOUSE KITCHEN CHOSE TO INSTALL A TIN CEILING BASED ON NINETEENTH-CENTURY DESIGNS. THE BACK-SPLASH TILES FEATURE WHIMSICAL KITCHEN AND COOKING-RELATED MOTIFS; THE LARGE SPOON WAS FOUND AT AN AUCTION.

Opposite: This rustic kitchen is nestled into the corner of a log cabin situated on an island just off the coast of Maine. The logs that line the ceiling, cabinets, and floor are from Great Ontario White Pine trees.

Above: A gleaming stainless teapot might appear too stand-out new in a room filled with pieces from the past, from the collection of pottery above the stove to the old wheel rim nestled into the window and the weathered logs that line the ceiling, but is actually quite at home beside a more old fashioned counterpart.

The Sophisticated Kitchen

If one were to coin a motto for the sophisticated kitchen, it would be the French saying: "*Une place pour chaque chose et chaque chose à sa place*," which translates to "A place for everything, and everything in its place." Here, the saying rings true, for the sophisticated kitchen is almost always completely built in. Cabinetry is flush with appliances and nothing sticks out from that one smooth plane, except perhaps an oversized professional range.

"Smooth" also describes these kitchens, which mostly feature smooth surfaces like stainless steel or glass, or highly buffed marble. In the sophisticated kitchen you won't find many textural elements like ornate cabinet doors. Most cabinets are completely flat for two reasons. First, the design aesthetic: since cabinetry usually takes up the most square footage of a kitchen, the look of the cabinetry will set the tone for the entire room. Simple cabinetry fits in with the unified, simple sophisticated look, and is easier on the eye. Second, flat cabinets are easier to clean since there are no nooks or decorative grooves for dust or food particles to settle.

Just as these kitchens are relatively void of decoration, they are also almost completely void of the usual kitchen clutter. Small appliances and kitchen gadgetry are hidden behind cabinets of stainless steel or perhaps pale wood. In some cases, oversized cabinets hide larger appliances like a washer/dryer or refrigerator. This type of design is ideal for loft living, where the entire home is a wide-open space, or for those whose kitchens are also their home office where employees and clients alike meet and sometimes eat.

Opposite: THE CHALLENGE IN THIS ROOM IS TO FIND THE APPLIANCES. AMONG THE ITEMS CLEVERLY CAMOUFLAGED BEHIND WOOD-PANELED SLIDING DOORS ARE A REFRIGERATOR (TO THE LEFT OF THE STOVE) AND STACKING WASHER/DRYER (TO THE RIGHT). A COOKTOP AND SINK ARE SET INTO THE ISLAND, SO THE USER CAN LOOK OUT ONTO THE REST OF THE APARTMENT WHILE PREPARING A MEAL. THE PEDESTALS OF THE ISLAND ARE COVERED IN BRUSHED ALUMINUM.

Above: A FREESTANDING TROUGHLIKE STRUCTURE HOUSES BOTH SINK AND COOKTOP, FREEING UP THE OPPOSITE COUNTER SPACE FOR FOOD PREPARATION. ADDITIONAL LIGHT IS PROVIDED BY A TRACK OUTFITTED WITH SMALL HALOGENS MOUNTED UNDERNEATH THE CABINETS. COOKING UTENSILS ARE STORED IN A CANISTER NEAR THE COOKTOP, AND POTS AND PANS HANG FROM A ROD THAT RUNS THE LENGTH OF THE BACK OF THE STRUCTURE.

Left: THIS KITCHEN IS MADE UP OF VERY SIMPLE, ANGULAR SHAPES IN THE CABINETRY, ECHOED IN THE RECTANGULAR EXPANSE OF WINDOWS AND THE SQUARE DINING TABLE, WHICH FOLDS OUT TO A LARGER SQUARE. THIN, ALUMINUM HORIZONTAL BLINDS COVER THE WINDOWS AND CREATE A SLEEK REFLECTIVE LIGHT PATTERN. **Below:** WOOD, MARBLE, AND STAINLESS STEEL ALL COEXIST IN A NEAT AND TIDY EUROPEAN KITCHEN. THE GENEROUSLY LONG CENTER ISLAND HAS A MARBLE TOP, MAKING IT SUITABLE FOR USE AS A PASTRY BOARD. THE ISLAND IS ALSO EQUIPPED WITH SEVERAL ELECTRICAL OUTLETS SO SMALL APPLIANCES CAN EASILY BE PLUGGED IN, USED AS NEEDED, AND THEN PUT AWAY.

Above: HAVING A COOKTOP SET INTO AN ISLAND IS A VERY UTILITARIAN DESIGN ELEMENT, FOR IT CREATES A CENTRAL PLACE FROM WHICH TO COOK SURROUNDED BY PREPARATION AREAS, AS SHOWN HERE. A STAINLESS STEEL HOOD PROVIDES REQUIRED VENTILATION AND MATCHES THE SLEEK REFRIGERATOR OF THE SAME MATERIAL. THE OVEN IS SET INTO THE WALL WITH A MICROWAVE POSITIONED ABOVE IN WHAT HAS BECOME A COMMON COMBINATION OF COOKING APPLIANCES.

Right: A FREESTANDING PORTABLE "ISLAND" WAS SPECIFIED FOR THIS ROOM SO THE OWNERS COULD HAVE THE FLEXIBILITY OF USING IT WHEREVER AN ADJACENT OR ADDITIONAL WORK SURFACE IS NEEDED, OR JUST AS A PLACE TO GRAB A QUICK SNACK. THE CABINETS ARE ASH VENEER PLYWOOD INSET WITH JUST ENOUGH GLASS TO MAKE THEM INTERESTING WITHOUT REVEALING TOO MUCH OF WHAT IS INSIDE.

Opposite: SOMETIMES THE SIMPLEST MATERIALS MAKE THE STRONGEST DESIGN STATEMENT, IN THIS CASE, THE PLYWOOD USED FOR THE SHARPLY ANGLED CABINETRY AND ISLAND. THE GREEN CABINETS ARE ALSO PLYWOOD, BUT WITH OLD FRONTS THAT WERE FOUND BY THE OWNERS AND PAINTED.

Above: THE OWNERS OF THIS KITCHEN LIKED THE IDEA OF INCORPORATING FRUIT SHAPES IN THE ROOM, HENCE THE BANANA-SHAPED ISLAND. MATCHING GRANITE COUNTERS AND BACKSPLASH CREATE CONTINUITY IN A KITCHEN WITH A LOT OF CURVES. **Right:** A LARGE PILLAR SERVES THE DUAL PURPOSE OF STRUCTURAL SUPPORT AND VISUALLY SEPARATING TWO DISTINCT AREAS OF THE KITCHEN: FOOD PREPARATION AND DINING. LIGHT FROM A LONE WINDOW SHINES UPON A GLASS BACKSPLASH AND A WALL OF GLASS-FRONTED SHELVES THAT PROVIDE OPEN SHELVING, BUT WITH ADDED FINGERPRINT PROTECTION FOR THE OBJECTS INSIDE.

Opposite: IF IT WEREN'T FOR THE SINK AND FAUCET, THIS ROOM COULD EASILY BE MISTAKEN FOR AN OFFICE INSTEAD OF A KITCHEN, ESPECIALLY WITH THE STAINLESS STEEL CABINETRY SET OFF THE MARBLE FLOOR AND LEATHER SWIVEL CHAIR. THE LOW CABINETRY ALLOWS FOR PLENTY OF LIGHT TO STREAM IN FROM BOTH THE WALL OF WINDOWS IN THE ADJACENT LIVING ROOM AND THE AREA ABOVE. **Above:** A PROBLEM WITH LOFT SPACES—OR A BLESSING, DEPENDING ON ONE'S POINT OF VIEW—IS THAT THERE IS NO REAL DISTINCTION BETWEEN ONE AREA OF THE SPACE AND THE NEXT. TO AMELIORATE THAT SITUATION, THE ARCHITECTS OF THIS LOFT ADDED A CIRCULAR, DROPPED DRUM TO THE CEILING THAT HOVERS OVER A PORTION OF THE KITCHEN AREA AND THE BREAKFAST TABLE. PANELS MADE OF GLASS AND FIBERBOARD (FOREGROUND) CAN SLIDE CLOSED TO PARTITION THE KITCHEN FROM MORE FORMAL AREAS OF THE HOME. CABINETS ARE ASH, STAINED DEEP EGGPLANT, COUNTERTOPS ARE BLACK GRANITE, AND THE BACKSPLASH IS FROSTED GLASS.

Below: AN EXTRA DEEP MARBLE SINK IS THE STAR OF THIS BUTLER'S PANTRY. THE ROOM HAS NO STOVE, BUT DOES FEATURE A SMALL REFRIGERATOR TO THE LEFT OF THE SINK AND A DISHWASHER TO THE RIGHT FOR CLEANING UP AFTER PARTIES. A WATER-FRIENDLY PIECE OF LIMESTONE WAS SET INTO THE HARDWOOD FLOOR IN FRONT OF THE SINK TO CATCH WATER BEFORE IT DRIPS ONTO THE FLOOR.

Above: THE ANGLES OF A CUSTOM-DESIGNED RANGE HOOD LEAD THE EYE TO THE TEXTURAL BACKSPLASH OF SMASHED TILES SET IN A RANDOM MOSAIC PATTERN. THE ZIGZAG STOVETOP GRID OF THE BURNERS ON THIS PROFESSIONAL QUALITY STOVE MAKES FOR A MORE EVEN DISTRIBUTION OF HEAT WHEN COOKING.

Above: THE CONCEPT OF THE "LIVING ROOM–KITCHEN" OR "GREAT ROOM" ENCOMPASSING BOTH LIVING ROOM AND KITCHEN HAS COME INTO FAVOR RECENTLY.

THIS ROOM MAKES THE CASE FOR THE "LIBRARY KITCHEN," AS IT IS A PERFECT SPACE IN WHICH TO ENJOY A BRANDY WHILE PERUSING A BOOK FROM THE NEARBY SHELVES.

THE RELATIVELY DARK MOOD SET BY THE CABINETRY AND BLACK APPLIANCES IS LIVENED UP BY CREAMY BEIGE WALLS.

Above: If the view into an adjacent room didn't suggest a home, one might think this was a restaurant kitchen. Indeed, almost everything in the room is industrial quality, from the appliances to the parts that make up the center island work area. The island is on wheels so it can easily be maneuvered to wherever it is needed most. Friends or family members can can pull up a stool to the counter to keep the chef company. The kitchen can be blocked off from the sun-drenched family room by pulling the folding screen closed. **Opposite:** For fans of the industrial looking kitchen, this room is a dream come true. Everything from cabinets to appliances to fixtures is either stainless steel or chrome. Diffused light flows in through a wall of glass blocks and reflects off the highly polished surfaces. Long, rectangular windows below the glass block wall push out to let fresh air in.

Above: Light wood tones with black accents are very Biedermeier yet the look in this kitchen is anything but. A glass-fronted cabinet for storing barware and stemware is conveniently located above a small bar sink set into a black granite countertop. A full-sized sink is positioned in the counter in the foreground, opposite the refrigerator.

Above: A SLATTED CEILING HIDES A COMPLEX LIGHTING SYSTEM OF FULL-SPECTRUM FLUORESCENT LIGHTS AND INCANDESCENT BULBS—NECESSARY BECAUSE THIS KITCHEN FACES NORTH—AND TIES IN WITH THE SLATS ON THE CUSTOM DESIGNED BENCHES. THE ARCHITECT CHOSE A FLUSH DESIGN FOR THE ASH-EDGED CHERRY VENEER CABINETS TO PREVENT THE KITCHEN FROM LOOKING TOO BUSY. TILES THAT LOOK LIKE VINTAGE ARTS AND CRAFTS PIECES BUT ARE ACTUALLY CONTEMPORARY HAND-PAINTED PIECES, LIVEN UP THE SPACE. **Right:** A PLACE FOR SERIOUS COOKING, THIS KITCHEN FEATURES NOT ONE BUT TWO OVENS AND A WALL FULL OF PROFESSIONAL-QUALITY REFRIGERATORS. A TRAY CEILING PROVIDES MORE FOCUSED TASK LIGHTING OVER A CENTER ISLAND, WHICH IS SET UP AS A PLACE TO PREPARE FOOD AS WELL AS SOCIALIZE. THE WROUGHT IRON OF THE BAR STOOLS COORDINATES NICELY WITH THE BLACK COUNTERS AND OTHER ACCENTS IN THE ROOM, WHILE THE RATTAN ADDS TEXTURE AND GIVES A CASUAL RELIEF FROM AN OTHERWISE SLEEK SPACE.

The Expressive Kitchen

Over the years, the kitchen has evolved from a room used for solely utilitarian purposes to a room where people congregate—not just for cooking, but for eating, visiting, and sometimes just lounging. As the functions of the kitchen have grown, the room has taken on a more personal tone, and as such is being decorated in ways that tap into the personalities of the owners, rendering the room, on the whole, more expressive.

Expressive kitchens reflect the passions of their owners. Collections are displayed either on open shelves or behind glass-paneled cabinetry. Works of art, or unusual materials like mesh screening, camouflage cabinet doors. Some rooms designed in the 1980s and 1990s are themed to look like they were wrought in the 1940s or 1950s with steel cabinetry, vintage linens and dining sets, and, in some cases, reconditioned appliances.

In addition, color, and lots of it, has found its way into the kitchen and designers are being anything but shy in the shades they choose. In some cases, color comes in the form of good old-fashioned paint used in newer, fresher ways. Decorative paint techniques like sponging, ragging, and stenciling are examples of this. For those without the time, money, or inclination to paint, color can come in the form of wallpaper that looks handpainted or stenciled, or in tiles that are available in almost every size, style, and price range imaginable.

Finally, whereas traditionally the kitchen consisted of appliances, cabinetry, and perhaps a table and chairs, many of today's kitchens are often part of a "great room" layout of one large open space that encompasses not only the kitchen, but also dining room and sometimes even living room areas. This type of expansion brings with it a whole new configuration of furniture and decorative accessories not normally associated with a kitchen, like upholstered chairs, bookshelves, and objets d'art.

Opposite: IT CAN BE A CHALLENGE TO FIND A SOLUTION FOR SECTIONING OFF ROOMS IN LARGE OPEN SPACES. IN THIS CASE, A FORMAL BUT FREESTANDING DOORWAY WAS BUILT INTO THE COUNTER SPACE TO SIGNAL ENTRANCE INTO THE KITCHEN AREA. THE BLACK ACCENTS ON OVERHEAD BEAMS AND CABINETS TIE IN WITH THE BLACK DOORFRAME, WHICH FEATURES SMALL, OPEN SHELVES ON EITHER SIDE FOR HOLDING VASES, STATUETTES, AND OTHER TREASURED OBJECTS. UNDERCOUNTER CABINETS ARE PAINTED TO RESEMBLE SHIRTS WITH BRIGHT RED COLLARS. THE LONG YELLOW SHELF TAKES A DRAMATIC DIP PROVIDING A NICHE FOR STORING COOKBOOKS.

Below: SQUARE TILES OF BROWN, BLACK, AND WHITE CREATE A DYNAMIC ZIGZAG PATTERN ON THE BACKSPLASH, AND THE SQUARE SHAPE THEME CARRIES OVER TO THE FLOOR AS WELL. RELIEF IS FOUND IN THE FORM OF RECTANGULAR SHAPES: ART HUNG ABOVE THE COUNTERS AND COLORED GLASS SET INTO A DOOR THAT SEPARATES THIS KITCHEN FROM AN ADJACENT BATHROOM. PLAYFUL HANDPRINTS PAINTED ON A FREESTANDING SCREEN REINFORCE THE SENSE OF FUN IN THE SPACE. **Opposite:** SOME SAY THE BEST WAY TO DECORATE A SMALL SPACE IS TO STICK WITH LIGHT COLORS. OBVIOUSLY, THE OWNER OF THIS KITCHEN DISAGREES. WALLS ARE PAINTED A BRIGHT COBALT BLUE AND STOCK CABINETS, WHICH WERE MOST PROBABLY WHITE AT THE OUTSET, NOW WEAR A SHADE OF TERRA-COTTA. CHRISTMAS LIGHTS STRUNG AROUND THE DOORWAY ADD ANOTHER FESTIVE TOUCH TO A LIVELY ROOM.

Above: A DECORATIVE PAINTER WAS CALLED IN TO STYLIZE THE OPEN KITCHEN IN THIS ART GALLERY. PARTICLEBOARD CABINETS GOT A WHOLE NEW LOOK, NAMELY A CUSTOM-COLORED THIN VENETIAN STUCCO FINISH APPLIED WITH A TROWEL THEN POLISHED TO BRING OUT THE SHINE IN THE PLASTER. THE CABINETS WERE THEN BUFFED WITH WAX. THE RESULT IS TRULY A WORK OF ART.

Opposite: WHAT A DIFFERENCE WALLPAPER CAN MAKE. WITHOUT IT, THIS KITCHEN WOULD STILL BE BEAUTIFUL, BUT ORDINARY. THE LIVELY KITCHENWARE PATTERN OF THE CORAL-COLORED PAPER SETS A WHIMSICAL TONE IN THIS ROOM BUT ALSO DRAWS ATTENTION TO THE WONDERFUL WHITE CABINETRY WITH ACCENT TRIM MOLDINGS AND A STATELY STOVE. **Above:** IN THIS REMODELED KITCHEN, ADJACENT BREAKFAST NICHE, AND MEDIA ROOM, THE CUSTOM CABINETS ARE STAINED MAPLE VENEER WITH SMALL, SQUARE METAL CORNER DETAILS AND CUSTOM-DESIGNED DRAWER PULLS. THE LIGHTING SCHEME, WHICH COMBINES TRACK HALOGENS WITH A DECORATIVE CHANDELIER, GIVES THE OWNERS A CHOICE BETWEEN TASK LIGHTING OR MORE AMBIENT LIGHT. THE SCULPTURAL WALL SCONCE, MADE OF SAND BLASTED PLEXIGLASS AND PATINATED BRASS WAS INSPIRED BY A LOVE OF GARDENING AND CREATED BY THE DESIGNERS.

Left: THE DESIGN OF THIS STOVE DATES BACK TO THE 1930S AND '40S, WHEN THE CONCEPT OF "COMBINATION RANGES" WAS FIRST INTRODUCED. COMBINATION RANGES BURNED TWO TYPES OF FUEL, USUALLY COAL AND GAS. SOME USED COAL AND ELECTRICITY. THIS STOVE HAS BEEN REVAMPED FOR USE IN CONTEMPORARY KITCHENS WITH THE ADDITION OF AUTOMATIC PILOT LIGHTS, BUT STILL MAINTAINS THE STYLE OF AN EARLIER ERA.

Above: The owners of a 1930s California home wanted to restore it in keeping with the era in which it was built. The kitchen restoration definitely fulfilled that goal, featuring cabinets with brushed steel pulls, vintage appliances, and art deco accessories including a built-in wall clock, a vintage cake plate, a straw holder, and a copper pitcher displayed in a glass-doored, round-edged, stainless steel cabinet.

Opposite: MESH SCREENING HAS RECENTLY EXPERIENCED A RESURGENCE AND IS NOW BEING UTILIZED IN VERY NON-TRADITIONAL WAYS. IN THIS KITCHEN, THE LOWER CABINETS FEATURE WOOD FRAME DOORS INSET WITH SCREENS AND THE PLUMBING, WHICH MIGHT NORMALLY BE HIDDEN BEHIND CABINETRY, IS INSTEAD ONLY PARTIALLY CONCEALED BY A SCREEN DOOR. THE USE OF MESH SCREENS HERE FUELS THE GENERAL COUNTRY PORCH FEELING OF THE SPACE WITH ITS VINTAGE TABLECLOTH AND RED AND WHITE FLOOR. **Above:** THIS 1950S KITCHEN WAS PUT TOGETHER ON AN UNBELIEVABLY MODEST BUDGET. STEEL CABINETS WERE PURCHASED FROM FRIENDS WHO WERE GOING TO TRASH THEM AND PAINTED WHITE. THE TABLE AND CHAIRS CAME FROM A YARD SALE, AND THE FLOOR IS BLANKETED WITH ASPHALT TILES. FRIENDS LIVING IN THE WESTERN PART OF THE UNITED STATES MADE THE COLORFUL TILES ENGRAVED WITH WESTERN MOTIFS LIKE COWBOYS AND CACTUSES, IN EXCHANGE FOR A TRIP TO THE EAST COAST. LURAYWARE, A POPULAR DISHWARE OF THE ERA, LINES SHELVED WALLS AND CREATES A COLORFUL DISPLAY THAT COMPLEMENTS THE TILES.

Below: APPLIANCES CAN BE DISGUISED IN A NUMBER OF WAYS. FOR THOSE WHO WANT PROFESSIONAL QUALITY APPLIANCES, BUT DON'T LOVE THE LOOK OF STAINLESS STEEL, THERE ARE OTHER OPTIONS. HERE, A BIG NAME REFRIGERATOR IS CLEVERLY DISGUISED BEHIND COPPER PANELS THAT FEATURE A CUSTOM PATTERN THAT SUPPORTS THE RUSTIC FEEL OF THE ROOM. THE COPPER OF THE REFRIGERATOER IS PICKED UP IN THE COPPER SINK BOWL AND RACK WITH COPPER POTS AND IS A NICE COMPLEMENT TO THE WARM YELLOW OF THE WALL-PAPER AND COBALT-BLUE PAINTED WOOD CHAIR.

Above: THIS KITCHEN IS A DESIGN PARADOX WITH ITS HEAVY, OLD, CAST-IRON STOVE WITH COPPER INLAYS JUXTAPOSED AGAINST AN AIRY LIGHT WOOD CABINET AND WALL-MOUNTED PLATE RACK. NATURAL LIGHT STREAMS IN THROUGH A WINDOW, CASTING SUNBEAMS OVER A LONG FARM TABLE AND PLATE RACK.

Above: Almost everything in this very blue room is as historic as the home it is housed in, an estate dating to the 1920s. The blue and white china is a classic and widely collected pattern. Fairly casual rush seat chairs are given a more formal look by the addition of a printed gold crest, and complementary gold accents. White cabinetry and flooring brighten the room while gingham seat cushions and a lively checked tablecloth lend a decidedly "country" flavor.

Kitchen Storage

Storage. It's a universal problem. No matter how large the room, the amount of stuff acquired over the years will always expand beyond the amount of available storage space. The key in avoiding such overflow situations is good planning. While it may seem perfectly reasonable to design a space around the items one already owns, it is even smarter to plan ahead and estimate storage for items that will become a part of the room in years to come. Some claim that having well-designed storage will actually cut down on the amount of time it takes to prepare a meal, because everything needed will be in its proper, readily accessible place.

One such place that is continuously popular is the kitchen island. While the concept of the island didn't appear in American kitchens until about the 1930s, it now enjoys a can't-live-without-it status—and for good reason.

The island provides an extra work surface, and, in some cases, can be moved around the room to where it is needed most. An island can be used as a barrier to distinguish between food preparation and eating areas. In terms of storage, the island provides an easy access spot to keep items used on a daily basis, including nonperishables, or can be used to display larger platters, ceramics or heirloom pieces.

However, innovative kitchen storage is not just for the stunning pieces. Even the most mundane items need to be stored and can be situated in their own special places. Thanks to the new flexibility in customizing cabinetry, even the basic sponge has a hidden resting place, as does almost any item imaginable. Built-ins can be configured to contain spice jars, utensils, oil and vinegar bottles, and even stepladders.

Opposite: THE CIRCULAR BREAKFAST NOOK IS SEPARATED FROM THE FORMAL KITCHEN AREA BY AN INTERESTING CURVED DIVIDER THAT SHOWCASES A COLLECTION OF POTTERY. DECORATIVE SHELVES ON THE RIGHT WALL AND ABOVE THE RANGE HOOD HOLD LARGER BOWLS, WHILE SMALLER OPEN SHELVES ON EITHER SIDE OF THE RANGE MAKE SPACE FOR SPICES AND GLASSWARE.

Above: FOR A COUPLE WHO SAYS THEIR FAMILY AND SOCIAL LIFE REVOLVE AROUND COOKING, A FAIRLY LARGE (19 × 28-FOOT [5.7 × 8.4M]) KITCHEN IS NEEDED, AS IS A CORRESPONDINGLY LARGE (8-FOOT [2.4M]) ISLAND. AT ONE END OF THIS ISLAND IS OPEN SHELVING FOR POTS AND PANS, THE OTHER END, SHOWN HERE, HAS A GRANITE COUNTERTOP WITH BUILT-IN SLOTS FOR KNIVES.

SIX PULL-OUT DRAWERS WITH GLASS FRONTS PROVIDE STORAGE FOR NON-PERISHABLES AND OTHER FREQUENTLY USED FOOD ITEMS. **Right:** FOR A PROFESSIONAL COOK AND RESTAURATEUR, STORAGE SOLUTIONS ARE SOMETIMES FOUND IN THE SIMPLEST WAYS. HERE, CABINETS AT ARM'S LENGTH FROM THE STOVE AND ADJACENT WORK SURFACE PROVIDE SPACE FOR STORING VARIOUS BAKING SHEETS, CUTTING BOARDS AND OTHER FLAT, OVERSIZED SURFACES, WHILE A PULL-OUT SHELF IS HOME TO A STACK OF BOWLS, PIE TINS, AND TART FORMS.

Above: THIS UNIT REPRESENTS NUMEROUS OPTIONS IN STORING KITCHEN SUPPLIES. IT DOESN'T GO ALL THE WAY TO THE CEILING, PROVIDING AN AREA TO STORE DECORATIVE BASKETS. A COLLECTION OF PAINTED DISHWARE IS DISPLAYED ON THE UNIT'S NUMEROUS SHELVES. THE BOTTOM PORTION HAS DRAWERS FOR STORING FLATWARE AND NAPKINS AND ENCLOSED CABINETS FOR HOUSING POTS AND PANS.

Above: SOMEONE ONCE SAID THAT "WHITE IS ALWAYS RIGHT" AND THE DESIGNER OF THIS KITCHEN WOULD MOST PROBABLY AGREE. THE ROOM IS OUTFITTED WITH PLENTY OF CABINETRY AND FEATURES A FEW EXTRAS LIKE A BUILT-IN FORTY-BOTTLE WINE RACK AND ELEGANT SHELVING WITH FRENCH DOORS FOR HOUSING A BEAUTIFUL COLLECTION OF CERAMICS.

Opposite: ONE SIDE OF THIS ISLAND FEATURES OPEN SHELVING FOR DISPLAYING SILVER AND COPPER HEIRLOOM PIECES AND OTHER KITCHEN ITEMS. THE SHAPE OF THE TWO CEILING ARCHES IS MIMICKED IN THE CURVED ISLAND AND THE DECORATIVE HANGING LIGHT FIXTURES.

Above: THE DISCREET DRAWERS ARE PERFECT FOR STORING EVERYTHING FROM UTENSILS TO DRY GOODS, OR PERHAPS THE REMOTE CONTROL FOR THAT TINY KITCHEN TV. THE FOUR DRAWERS GIVE A BASIC SIDE-BY-SIDE, OPEN-CABINET STYLE A NEW LOOK, SOMEWHAT JAPANESE IN FEELING, AND ACCENTED BY INTERESTING BLACK VERTICAL PULLS. **Opposite:** AN IMPOS-ING WALL OF CABINETS LINES A STORAGE PANTRY IN A HOME DESCRIBED AS A CLASSIC GRAND COTTAGE IN MAINE. THE CABINETS RUN NOT JUST THE LENGTH, BUT ALSO THE HEIGHT OF THE WALL, WITH DECORATIVE CROWN MOLDING TOUCHING THE CEILING. AN IMPRESSIVE ARRAY OF CHINA AND STEMWARE IS EASILY ACCOMMODATED IN THE CABINETRY OF THIS HOME, WHICH IS NOW A BED-AND-BREAKFAST.

Opposite: THOSE WITH A PASSION FOR STAINLESS STEEL WILL FIND THAT THE RANGE OF THIS MATERIAL IS NOT LIMITED TO JUST BACKSPLASHES OR APPLIANCES. METAL CABINETS, MOST COMMONLY USED FOR HOSPITALS OR DOCTOR'S OFFICES, ARE GAINING POPULARITY FOR KITCHEN USE. BUT BE SURE YOU HAVE THE BUDGET BEFORE FALLING IN LOVE WITH THE LOOK. CABINETRY OF THIS KIND IS USUALLY CUSTOM FITTED AND CAN BE VERY EXPENSIVE, NOT TO MENTION HIGH MAINTENANCE (THINK FINGERPRINTS!). **Above:** WHEN THIS ROOM WAS RENOVATED, THE CHALLENGE WAS TO CREATE PLENTY OF ROOM FOR STORAGE ON A BUDGET THAT DID NOT ALLOW FOR FULL-FLEDGED CABINETRY. THE SOLUTION: METAL SHELVING, AS IN THE KIND COMMONLY FOUND IN STOCK ROOMS, SPRAYED WITH METALLIC GRAY AUTOMOTIVE PAINT AND AN ISLAND WITH THE SAME OPEN SHELVING ON THE BOTTOM WITH A GRANITE TOP TO MATCH THE COUNTERS.

Below: A FREESTANDING CABINET OR ARMOIRE IS A WELCOME ADDITION TO A KITCHEN SPACE FOR SEVERAL REASONS. IT PROVIDES STORAGE, IN THIS CASE, FOR A COLLECTION OF VINTAGE CERAMICS. IT ALSO BREAKS UP THE SOMETIMES TOO-UNIFIED LOOK OF BUILT-IN CABINETRY, AND, WHEN PAINTED A BRIGHT COLOR, IS SURE TO LIVEN UP ANY ROOM.

Above: FOR THE KITCHEN IN WHICH EVERYTHING MUST BE HIDDEN, COMPLEX CABINETRY CONFIGURATIONS BECOME ESSENTIAL. HERE, FIVE SHELVES INDIVIDUALLY SLIDE OUT FOR OPTIMAL STORAGE OF, AND EASY ACCESS TO, DINNERWARE AND BARWARE.

Above: OPEN CABINETRY LOOKS ESPECIALLY ELEGANT WHEN STOCKED WITH WHITE CHINA AND CREAMWARE, CRYSTAL, AND A FEW WELL-SELECTED SILVER PIECES. THIS UNIT IS TRULY OPEN, IN THAT IT IS BACKED NOT BY WOOD BUT BY WHITE TILES. THE STAGGERED SHELVING OF THE CENTER SECTION ADDS VISUAL INTEREST AND ALLOWS TALLER ITEMS LIKE A PAIR OF CANDLESTICKS AND A PEDESTAL-STYLE FRUIT BOWL.

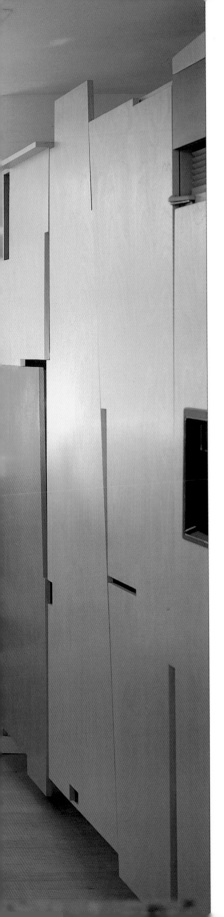

Left: An island with built-in cabinetry is not a new concept. However, this extended island, with bench seating at the far end, features drawers and cabinets that look ill-fitted. This was very calculated, however, for the gaps between the units function as drawer and cabinet pulls (notice the cabinetry is devoid of any hardware). Units are differentiated by color. **Below:** The wonderful geometric patterns of these freestanding cabinets are emphasized by the curvilinear objects kept inside them. The upper units have no hardware and therefore give the illusion of being completely open when the doors actually have glass panels. Lower cabinets are a mix of traditional shelving with long, thin drawers perfect for storing flatware and linens. The grid pattern of the curved stainless steel chair backs completes the geometric theme.

Above, Left: An elegantly subtle storage solution is found here in the form of a bench. The top and bottom parts are hinged and open out, revealing storage for glasses, mugs, bowls, plates, and even flatware. **Above, Right:** This photo illustrates that in today's kitchen, there truly is a place for everything. The cabinetry was custom designed to hold a variety of pedestrian kitchen objects, including sponges and even a step stool. Inside the far door, a slide-out surface holds a heavy-duty mixer.

Opposite: This kitchen demonstrates how to most efficiently use a small space. Namely, plenty of cabinet space, with glass doors for storing dishes and glasses, and under-the-counter cabinets for pots and pans. The warm stain of the cabinetry gives the room a cozy, but not cramped, feeling. A rectangular window is almost hidden above the cooktop and behind the hood, but provides an interesting view for anyone working at the stove.

PART THREE
DINING AREAS

INTRODUCTION

The ritual of eating together has to be one of the most common—yet complex—activities mankind has yet devised. It gives us the opportunity to spend time with our families, rest from work, and socialize with friends. In fact, many of the events in our lives revolve around food, from prosaic family meals to milestones marked by celebratory repasts to savory holiday feasts. These are instances that we will always remember.

Given the monumental importance that eating has in our lives, it is not surprising that all sorts of areas have evolved in our homes to accommodate this activity. The sites at which we dine are many and varied, and some residences have more than one area designated for this purpose. There are formal dining rooms, eat-in kitchens, quaint breakfast nooks, and dining areas carved out of libraries; the great room, a relatively new innovation that is supplanting the formal living room, often incorporates an eating area; and many of us have also found spaces on our terraces and patios for dining.

But given the history of dining, it is clear that society as a whole has made the most of the experience only in contemporary times. Although dining was an extraordinary affair for the upper classes during previous centuries, it was a far more humble experience for the masses. Upper-class males reclined on couches while dining in ancient Assyria, Samaria, Phoenicia, Greece, and Rome; this practice limited fine dining to groups that were small and exclusive, since not many couches could fit in a room. And at the beginning of the European Middle Ages, an aristocratic household would typically have a spacious central hall where servants would eat while watched by their lord. The master would eventually withdraw to dine in private with his companions, and the practice of eating in chambers away from the lower orders evolved.

Rooms designed for the sole purpose of dining were not built into middle-class homes until the seventeenth century. When this type of space evolved, furnishings specific to the room quickly followed suit. For the first time,

Opposite: With lush floral slipcovers over half of its chairs, this Colonial dining room sports a summery look throughout the seasons. An airy chandelier, a bountiful floral centerpiece, and blue-and-white checkered drapes complete the pretty picture and make dining here seem like a formal indoor picnic.

distinctive tables that were stationary, and meant only for eating, were built. Prior to that, trestles and boards were constantly being set up and dismantled in whatever space could accommodate them. These temporary arrangements were adorned, however, with splendid cloths—a procedure, in fact, that originated the practice of dressing the table.

Along with the dining room came many other innovations, such as place settings, silver, glassware and linens as we know them today, elegant dining chairs, sideboards, buffets, breakfronts, and cupboards. The concept that functional objects could also be decorative, even fanciful, began to take hold, and soon whole industries revolving around the accoutrements of dining sprang up. By the mid-nineteenth century, the dining room was laden with layers of elaborate gear. There were pieces of cutlery for every kind of food, as well as plates, serving pieces, and glasses in every size for every imaginable course. As specialized forms evolved for cheese, fruit, fish, shellfish, meat, salad, and soup, a place setting of silver or china could include a dozen different pieces. Cabinetry to store these pieces proliferated and even became a necessity for a well-appointed room.

It is important to remember, though, that all these accessories were designed to grace the dining table, which was—

Above: Despite the fact that this adobe room has rustic beamed ceilings and a terra-cotta tile floor, it is furnished with Queen Anne chairs, a simple provincial trestle table, an Empire love seat, and baroque wrought-iron fixtures embellished with flamboyant crystal balls—all of which provide a welcome surprise. The room has an ageless quality, seeming contemporary and archaic at the same time due to the almost magical blend of elements.

and still is—the focal point of a dining area. Since everything revolves around this one crucial piece of furniture, it has traditionally been a substantial—and special—piece.

The first stationary dining tables, crafted in heavy dark woods polished to perfection, reflected the style of their day. They were usually rectangular, both to accommodate strict hierarchical seating distinctions and to suit the oblong shapes of the rooms in those days. The furnishings that surrounded the dining table matched in terms of style and scale, for the dining room was a very formal space. In fact, it retained its starched demeanor until quite recently, when the nature of formal dining spaces changed and contemporary design popularized the concept of "the big blend."

Today, dining tables continue to take center stage, but they no longer adhere to one specific shape or style. Moreover, they are not always placed in formal spaces. Personal preference is far more important than social convention; thus, there are no rules to dictate the style and dimensions of our tables. If anything, taste and common sense help determine the type of table chosen. Rectangular tables work better for large groups, while those that are round are far more democratic. Plus tables that expand and contract, such as those with leaves or clever foldout surfaces, provide far more versatility than tables that are truly stationary.

And just as personal preference leads us to pick certain tables, it leads us to array our dining areas as we please. Many factors influence this process, starting with the size of the space, how it has to function, and an individual's taste and sense of decorum. Some dining areas are still formal, while others are casual, relaxed, and even full of surprise. It is possible to recreate a perfect period room, be it a stately Federal or Empire interior or a sleek Art Deco or Modernist milieu, or produce a fantastic space that incorporates all sorts of decorative elements in an eclectic blend. Somewhere in between fall rooms that reflect regional or ethnic styling.

Ultimately, a dining area must be an inviting space designed for sharing, since eating is an activity that often takes place in the company of others. Dining is an entertaining and fulfilling social experience, and the setting for such an endeavor should be comfortable, engaging, and ideally, stimulate the appetite and conversation. Given such a space, who wouldn't want to linger around a table for hours at a time?

FORMAL DINING

In 1879, an anonymous aristocrat wrote in an English manners book that "dinner parties rank first among all entertainments." Considering the marvelous times to be had—both intellectually and gastronomically—around a table, this observation is astute. Moreover, it reminds us that a dinner party demands a stage of its own on which it can unfold.

The notion of a singular room devoted entirely to dining became most firmly established as a standard in the European household during the second half of the nineteenth century, at just about the same time that this blue blood was advocating the merits of the dinner party. It was a fortuitous development, for what better way is there to enjoy the diversion of dining than in an alluring room outfitted for the occasion?

A grand table is like a mannequin that can be dressed many ways. Thanks to its proportions, it already anchors the room, but it receives its character from the furnishings and accessories around it. Pristine linens bring it starched propriety, while vibrant fabrics make it festive. Chairs add attitude, whether it is the refinement offered by traditional Chippendales or the "edge" induced by avant-garde designs. Other furnishings, such as breakfronts and sideboards, remind us of the utilitarian aspects of dining and its many necessary accessories.

Enjoying a dinner party in a formal dining room is only half the fun. Indeed, picking and choosing all the accoutrements for the space can be just as mesmerizing.

Opposite: STARK SIMPLICITY MAKES THIS ROOM STUNNING, ALLOWING ITS CAREFULLY PRESERVED ARCHITECTURAL ELEMENTS TO TAKE CENTER STAGE. THE WAINSCOTING, CORNICES, AND WINDOW CASEMENTS LITERALLY JUMP OFF THE WALLS IN PURE WHITE, WHILE THE FLAT PARTS OF THE SURFACE ARE GIVEN DEPTH WITH A COAT OF DEEP GRAY PAINT. FURNISHING THIS SPECTACULAR SPACE WITH JUST A TABLE AND CHAIRS SHOWS REMARKABLE RESTRAINT, BUT PAYS OFF WITH THE DRAMATIC IMPACT EVOKED BY SUCH MINIMALISM. **Above:** A FORMAL SEVENTEENTH-CENTURY DINING ROOM IN THE ENGLISH COUNTRYSIDE WOULD HAVE LOOKED VERY MUCH LIKE THIS, RIGHT DOWN TO THE LOW CEILINGS, BANISTER-BACK CHAIRS, ORIENTAL CARPET, AND ELABORATE CANDELABRA. THANKS TO THE FIREPLACE, THE SPACE FEELS IMPOSING AND INTIMATE AT THE SAME TIME—A RARE BALANCE IN ANY SETTING.

Opposite: THIS AIRY DINING ROOM TAKES MUCH FROM CLASSIC REGENCY STYLING, STARTING WITH THE DINING TABLE AND CHAIRS. SINCE ALL PIECES FROM THIS PERIOD HAVE MUCH IN COMMON, MIXING TWO TYPES OF CHAIRS LOOKS QUITE ELEGANT INSTEAD OF DISCORDANT, AND EVEN GIVES THE SETTING A DIS-CREET TOUCH OF EXCITEMENT. THE WALLS BORROW THE MOST FROM THE PERIOD, WHEN LARGE PLAIN SURFACES WERE FREQUENTLY PAINTED A SINGLE COLOR AND COVERED WITH SUBTLE STENCILED PATTERNS. HOWEVER, THE USE OF A COORDINATING BORDER EMBLA-ZONED WITH EPIGRAMS TRANSPORTS THE ROOM INTO TODAY'S TIMES.

Above: EVEN THOUGH IT IS TUCKED AWAY IN A CORNER, A SURREALISTIC GRANDFATHER CLOCK STANDS WATCH IN THIS ROOM AND GIVES IT ATTITUDE. WHILE OTHER ELEMENTS APPEAR AT FIRST GLANCE TO BE MINIMAL, THE SPACE ACTUALLY EMPLOYS SPECIAL PIECES TO MAXIMUM EFFECT. DESPITE SEEMINGLY STRAIGHTFORWARD LINES, THE DINING SET RELATES TO THE CLOCK WITH ITS SUBTLY ECCENTRIC CHAIRS. AND A WHITE VASE THAT ECHOES THE CHAIRS' FAN-SHAPED BACKS SERVES AS A COUNTERPOINT TO THE ALL-BLACK TABLE SURFACE. FINALLY, A CONTEMPORARY PAINTING THAT COMBINES THE HUES OF THE ROOM PULLS THE VARIOUS COMPONENTS TOGETHER.

Above: A WOOD DINING SET WITH STRONG, CHUNKY LINES LOOKS HIGHLY REFINED AS A "BLOND." ALTHOUGH IT TAKES ITS CUES FROM THE SENSIBLE AND SERIOUS MISSION MOVEMENT, A WARDROBE OF RUFFLED SKIRTS IMBUES IT WITH A TOUCH OF WIT AND SOFTENS ITS SOBER PROFILE. THE SET PROVIDES AN INTERESTING CONTRAST TO THE DARK WOOD FLOOR AND TROLLEY. **Right:** BOLD GEOMETRIC SHAPES PUNCTUATE THIS ROOM, GIVING IT A COMMANDING AIR. BUT BILLOWING DRAPES, UPHOLSTERED CHAIRS, AND FRESH FLOWERS TONE DOWN THE SHARP ANGLES THAT DOMINATE THE SPACE, MAKING IT SEEM A LITTLE MORE DELICATE.

Opposite: In this surreal dining room, caricatures of tradition mingle with the real thing, producing a remarkably sophisticated and cohesive effect. The tenets of Queen Anne styling are stretched in the exaggerated lines of the blond wood pieces, which clearly do not take themselves too seriously: tall pottery pokes out over the top of the cabinet, the chair looks lopsided, and the frame lacks a picture. But when paired with authentic antique elements—namely a Victorian spiral-leg table base, Empire chairs, and a primitive bench—these pieces make the room engaging.

Right: A breathtaking alcove outfitted in icy white makes a spectacular spot for dining, especially when blessed with the stunning backdrop of a lake. In this case, though, the vista was actually a mixed blessing since it rendered the space somewhat cold and pristine. Easy chairs placed around the table make the nook more cozy, while pale green paint provides an additional softening effect.

Left, top: THIS TINY DINING ALCOVE SPORTS MANY ELEMENTS OF BAROQUE STYLING. THE MASSIVE FORM OF THE ARMOIRE, WITH ITS SWELLING CURVES AND LACQUERED VENEER, DOMINATES THE ROOM, WHICH IS ACCENTUATED BY ROD-HUNG CURTAINS (AN INNOVATION OF THE PERIOD). TO OFFSET THE ROOM'S SMALL SIZE AND GIVE IT THE ILLUSION OF SPACIOUSNESS, THE FAR WALL IS PANELED WITH MIRRORS WHILE THE OTHER WALLS, ALONG WITH THE CEILING, ARE PAINTED AN AIRY SHADE OF YELLOW (ALSO POPULAR DURING THE BAROQUE PERIOD). BUT A CLEVER MIX OF OTHER PERIOD PIECES, ACCENTED BY INDONESIAN TEXTILES, BRINGS THIS ROOM INTO THE ERA OF JET TRAVEL.

Left, bottom: THIS TEX-MEX MILIEU OWES MUCH TO OTHER INFLUENCES. THE CHAIRS ARE PURE ADIRONDACK, THE HARVEST TABLE IS RIGHT OUT OF THE MIDWEST, AND THE LAMP IS ARTS AND CRAFTS. BUT THE NATIVE AMERICAN TEXTILE AND POTTERY, COUPLED WITH AN ANTIQUE MEXICAN SERAPE AND A BEAMED CEILING, CEMENT THE AMBIENCE OF THE ROOM AS SOUTHWESTERN.

Opposite: IT IS HARD TO IMAGINE A WONDERFUL ROOM TOTALLY WASHED IN ORANGE, BUT THIS DINING AREA MANAGES TO BE EARTHY, WARM, WITTY, AND UNDENIABLY THAT HUE ALL AT THE SAME TIME. PART OF THE SUCCESS OF THE MILIEU IS OWED TO THE MELLOW TONE-ON-TONE APPROACH EMPLOYED IN THE PALETTE, WHICH RANGES FROM A SUNNY TANGERINE TO A RICH TERRA-COTTA. BUT OTHER SLY DEVICES, SUCH AS COMIC SLIPCOVERS THAT MAKE THE CHAIRS LOOK LIKE COURT JESTERS AND A FLASHY FIXTURE WITH FAUX-SKIN SHADES, CLUE US IN ON THIS ROOM'S REAL AIM, WHICH IS TO ENTERTAIN.

Above: HERE, REGAL SPANISH COLONIAL FURNISHINGS ARE ENHANCED BY STARK WHITE ADOBE WALLS, WHICH SHOW OFF THE INKY MAHOGANY PIECES TO PERFECTION. A VIVID TRADITIONAL NATIVE AMERICAN RUG ADDS COLOR TO THE SETTING, WHILE THE CEILING, WITH ITS DARK WOOD BEAMS AND STENCILED GEOMETRIC MOTIF, FUSES THE CULTURAL ASPECTS OF THE SPACE. HOWEVER, THE ROOM IS NOT WITHOUT ITS IDIOSYNCRASIES: NEOCLASSICAL DORIC COLUMNS FLANKING THE DOOR ARE TOTALLY OUT OF PLACE BUT WORK, THANKS TO THEIR MOTTLED TONES AND THE CARVED MAHOGANY CORNICE THEY SUPPORT. **Opposite:** HERE, ELEGANT UPHOLSTERED DINING CHAIRS WITH BOX-PLEATED SKIRTS BRING SOBRIETY TO AN AUDACIOUS ALUMINUM TABLE, JUST AS WHITE GLOVES WOULD TONE DOWN A SHOWY PAIR OF PATENT LEATHER SHOES. OTHER SPLASHY ELEMENTS—NAMELY THE CHAMPAGNE STAND AND THE BRIGHT SHADE OF RED SANDWICHED BETWEEN THE WAINSCOTING AND MOLDING—DO NOT APPEAR OVERWHELMING THANKS TO CAREFUL EDITING AND BALANCE.

Opposite: EXCESS REIGNS SUPREME IN THIS ROOM, WHICH IS STARTLING ON ACCOUNT OF ITS BOLD USE OF COLOR, PATTERN, AND PROPORTION. MASSIVE CHINOISERIE PIECES, SUCH AS THE BREAKFRONT AND DINING SET, ARE SURROUNDED BY A COCOON OF COLORS AND PATTERNS THAT PLAY OFF THE RED AND GOLD TONES IN THESE FURNISHINGS. THE WALL TREATMENT, WHICH CONSISTS OF A PATCHWORK APPROACH THAT FUSES SQUARES OF DIFFERENT-PATTERNED PAPERS ALL ON THE SAME SURFACE, IS A MOST NOVEL DEVICE THAT CAN BE DUPLICATED IN OTHER SETTINGS.

Right: COMBINING A QUILTED TABLE SKIRT, TEXTURED SLIPCOVERS, AND FLOCKED CANVAS DRAPES WAS A DARING MOVE THAT PAID OFF. EACH OF THE TEXTILES IS RICH IN ITS OWN RIGHT, BUT TOGETHER THEY BECOME DOWNRIGHT OPULENT AS THEY PLAY OFF ONE ANOTHER. THIS SAME LOOK CAN BE DUPLICATED WITH SIMILAR FABRICS THAT ARE FAR MORE HUMBLE, SUCH AS A MOVER'S QUILT OR A PRINTED CHINTZ.

TASTICAL NEO-GOTHIC SETTING, THE BUILT-IN WALNUT CABINET, WHICH WAS DESIGNED TO RESEMBLE THE EXTERIOR OF A GOTHIC BUILDING, IS ACTUALLY A STRUCTURAL DEVICE THAT HIDES THE ROOM'S ONLY WINDOW, WHICH OVERLOOKS AN UNAPPEAL-ING FIRE ESCAPE. NATURAL LIGHT, HOWEVER, IS PERMITTED TO SHINE IN FROM THE GLASS EXPANSE AT THE TOP OF THE UNIT, AND A TROMPE L'OEIL SKY COVERS THE CEILING, THEREBY OPENING UP THE SPACE AND MASKING THE FACT THAT THE CEILING IS ACTUALLY QUITE LOW. SINCE THIS BUSY BACKDROP CALLS FOR VERY LITTLE FURNITURE, ONLY THE BARE NECESSITIES HAVE BEEN INCORPORATED. A GOTHIC-STYLE TABLE, WHICH USED TO BE THE PROP OF AN OPERA COMPANY, WAS DIS-TRESSED TO LOOK LIKE THE REAL THING, WHILE TAPESTRY FROM A FABRIC STORE WAS MADE INTO A REGAL TABLECLOTH. TURN-OF-THE-CENTURY FRENCH METAL GARDEN CHAIRS MAKE A PERFECT COUNTER-POINT TO THE MASSIVE PIECE.

Above: EMPIRE ROOMS WERE DRENCHED IN GILT AND LUXURIOUSLY SWATHED WITH GLEAMING SILK AND TAFFETA TO EMULATE MAGNIFICENT MILITARY TENTS. THIS DINING ROOM, WITH ITS DRAPED WALLS, LAVISH GOLD PASSEMENTERIE, HUGE GILT-FRAMED MIRROR, AND RUG EMBLAZONED WITH MEDALLIONS, RECREATES THE PERIOD SO STUNNINGLY THAT THE SIMPLICITY OF THE DINING SET GOES UNNOTICED. THOUGH CLEARLY NOT EMPIRE, THE TABLE AND CHAIRS FIT RIGHT IN AND ARE MADE FAR MORE GRAND BY THEIR OPULENT SURROUNDINGS.

Above: NOTHING CONVEYS THE ESSENCE OF STYLE BETTER THAN A SKILLFUL BLEND. HERE, AN ODD COUPLING BECOMES A STELLAR MATCH, AS A SPACE FITTED WITH SLEEK CONTEMPORARY BUILT-IN CABINETRY HOUSES A MASSIVE VICTORIAN DINING TABLE. THE SUBTLETY OF THE ROOM, WITH ITS UNDERSTATED BUT QUIETLY ELEGANT VENEERS, IS NOT ONLY BALANCED BY THE FLASHY TABLE—IT THRIVES ON THE FLAMBOYANCE. SPARTAN WOVEN RATTAN CHAIRS AROUND THE TABLE PROVIDE JUST THE RIGHT COUNTERPOINT, BRINGING THE STRIKING PIECE UP-TO-DATE.

Left: A BUILT-IN MISSION-STYLE SIDEBOARD DID NOT INHIBIT THE DESIGNER OF THIS ROOM, WHO CONTRASTED ETHEREAL TROMPE L'OEIL MURALS OF THE ITALIAN COUNTRYSIDE AND A ROMANTIC AUBUSSON RUG WITH CONTEMPORARY ITALIAN AVANT-GARDE FURNISHINGS. THE GLASS TABLE AND ITS ACCOMPANYING CHAIRS ARE SO SPARE AND MINIMAL THAT THEY ALLOW THE BEAUTY OF THE RUG TO SHINE THROUGH. ALTHOUGH THE COMPONENTS OF THIS ROOM ARE DISPARATE, THEY HAVE BEEN HARMONIOUSLY WOVEN TOGETHER.

Above: A ROOM CAN SAY "COUNTRY" BUT STILL SPEAK THE SAME LANGUAGE AS ITS PEERS IN SLICKER SETTINGS.

HERE, THE ARCHITECTURAL ELEMENTS OF A NEW ENGLAND DINING ROOM GIVE OFF A GENERAL SENSE OF COUNTRY STYLING.

BUT OUTFITTING THE SPACE WITH TRAPPINGS FROM THE GEORGIAN PERIOD—NAMELY A SPLENDID BURNISHED DINING SET IN THE

CHIPPENDALE FASHION, A GRACEFUL CHANDELIER, AND AN ORIENTAL CARPET—DRESSES UP THE FOLKSY BRICK-LINED HEARTH.

THESE FURNISHINGS WOULD BE DIGNIFIED IN ANY SPACE; HERE, THEY MAKE THE DINING ROOM DECOROUS.

Informal Dining

While some find eating to be one of life's greatest pleasures, there is a compulsory side to this activity: we either do it or die. So eat we do, day in and day out, in a multitude of informal settings. Some people steal meals in a kitchen alcove, while others sit down with the whole household in spacious rooms. The challenge is not necessarily finding a spot for routine meals; it is making an eating environment inviting and comfortable enough for daily use.

There are many ways to make an informal dining area much more than merely routine. A good place to start is with a spectacular table, which does not have to be costly, ceremonious, or even conventional. The humble harvest table thrives just as well in an informal setting as

do its showier brethren, and there is even room for dining surfaces that are atypical or eccentric. What matters is how the table works in its environment. Can it accommodate all the members of a family; does it suit the space; and is it going to be easy to maintain?

Other basics to bring to an informal dining area include comfortable chairs, a manageable circulation pattern, plenty of storage, and good lighting. But it is the extras that make the space great. An imaginative paint job goes a long way in making the room engaging, as do novel fabric treatments, such as slipcovers or a table skirt. Sometimes that one special touch makes the otherwise mundane space we eat in every day remarkable.

Opposite: REPRESENTING SIMPLER TIMES, A BEAUTIFULLY WEATHERED HARVEST TABLE CAN IMBUE A ROOM WITH THE INNOCENCE OF A PAST ERA. HERE, A QUAINT FRINGED CLOTH DEFTLY COVERS ONLY PART OF SUCH A TABLE, ALLOWING THE NATURAL BEAUTY OF THE WOOD TO BE ENJOYED. BRIGHTLY PAINTED CHAIRS, MANIFESTING A SLIGHTLY WEATHERED LOOK THAT BLENDS IN READILY WITH THE RUSTIC TABLE, ADD A SPLASH OF FESTIVITY TO THE SETTING. A SUBDUED FLORAL CARPET AND SUBTLY STENCILED WALLS FURTHER ENHANCE THE MODEST TABLE WITHOUT OVERSHADOWING IT.

Above: A BEAUTIFUL NATIVE AMERICAN RUG AND INTRICATE MOLDINGS GIVE THIS SPACE A SERIOUS DEMEANOR, BUT WHITE WICKER CHAIRS AND TABLECLOTHS RESEMBLING PICNIC BLANKETS HELP THE ROOM TO "LIGHTEN UP." THESE PLAYFUL ELEMENTS LIBERATE THE ROOM FROM THE CONSTRAINTS OF ADHERING TO A SPECIFIC STYLE, THEREBY LENDING THE AREA A CAREFREE SPIRIT.

Above: EIGHTEENTH-CENTURY COUNTRY STYLING HAS BEEN EVOKED WITH STUNNING RESULTS IN THIS INVITING MILIEU, WHERE AN ABUNDANCE OF WINDOWS GIVES THE SPACE A REFRESHING FEELING. THE FURNISHINGS, ALL OF WHICH ARE NEW EXCEPT FOR THE PLANK DINING TABLE, HAVE BEEN CHOSEN WITH EXTREME ACUMEN TO CREATE AN OVERALL PERIOD LOOK. TWO-TONE WINDSOR CHAIRS, COMPLETE WITH CONTEMPORARY FLOURISHES ON THE ARMS, AND A CHANDELIER WITH SOFTENING SHADES ADD THE SAME KIND OF ELEGANCE TO THE ROOM THAT ORIGINALS WOULD. **Opposite:** THANKS TO A MINIMAL USE OF FURNISHINGS AND COLOR, THE ARCHITECTURAL SPLENDOR OF THIS SPACE GRABS CENTER STAGE. THE FEW PIECES THAT ARE EMPLOYED MAKE KEY CONTRIBUTIONS TO THE SETTING: UNUSUAL WHITE CHAIRS WITH CASTORS, WHICH ADD TO THE CASUAL TONE OF THE ROOM, BLEND IN WITH THE BRIGHT WHITENESS OF THE SPACE'S STRUCTURAL ELEMENTS, WHILE THE CHAIRS' CURVED BACKS PROVIDE CONTRAST TO THE CRISP ARCHITECTURE. MEANWHILE, THE PALE WOOD TABLE BLENDS SEAMLESSLY INTO THE FLOOR AND BEARS A DARK BORDER THAT MIRRORS THE ONE BELOW.

Above, left: THIS SUNNY DINING AREA DEFINES CASUAL ELEGANCE IN EVERY WAY. A WOODEN FARM TABLE PAIRED WITH LINEN-SLIPCOVERED CHAIRS AND DRESSED WITH FINE TABLE LINENS, ORNATE FLATWARE, AND SILVER CANDLESTICKS IS AT ONCE RELAXED YET READY FOR COMPANY. LIKEWISE, THE ORIENTAL RUG ADDS A MORE FORMAL TOUCH THAT IS BALANCED BY THE SIMPLICIITY OF THE RUSTIC CHANDELIER, CURTAIN TREATMENT, AND WOODEN CHEST OF DRAWERS.

Above, right: A FEW SIMPLE BUT UNUSUAL FABRIC TREATMENTS ENHANCE THIS DINING AREA. BOX PLEATS ADD A TOUCH OF WHIMSY TO THE STRAIGHTFORWARD SLIPCOVERS, AND A DIAPHANOUS DRAPE BRINGS ADDITIONAL SOFTNESS TO THE DECOR. A RICE-PAPER FIXTURE CASTING A BURNISHED GLOW ECHOES THE SHAPE OF THE TABLE BELOW AS WELL AS THE HUE OF THE GOSSAMER WINDOW COVERING. COMBINED, THESE ELEMENTS CREATE AN INTIMATE AND NURTURING ENVIRONMENT.

Left: A SUBTLE MOTIF CAN DEMONSTRATE TREMENDOUS DECORATIVE POWER. HERE, A SIMPLE CARVED STAR-IN-A-CIRCLE DESIGN APPEARS ON THE BACKBOARD OF EACH CHAIR, AS WELL AS ON DECORATIVE BRACKETS EMBELLISHING THE CORNERS OF THE ROOM. CREATING AN OVERALL TEX-MEX APPEAL, THE MOTIF SETS THE TONE FOR THE REST OF THE FURNISHINGS. SUDDENLY ELEMENTS THAT COULD REFLECT SEVERAL DIFFERENT STYLES— SUCH AS A COLLECTION OF POTTERY, A TILED HARVEST TABLE, AND A WEATHERED CUPBOARD—SEEM DECIDEDLY SOUTHWESTERN.

Opposite: IN THIS COZY DINING ROOM, THE TABLE WAS THE INSPIRATION FOR THE SURROUNDING DECOR, WHICH BOASTS A SUPERB FAUX PAINT JOB THAT EMULATES THE TABLE'S BEAUTIFULLY VARIEGATED MARBLE SURFACE. SIMPLE WOOD CHAIRS AND A SISAL RUG TONE DOWN THE OPULENCE AND FORMALITY SUGGESTED BY MARBLE, WHILE A BOLD SAUCERLIKE FIXTURE AND FRENCH DOORS BOASTING A DYNAMIC SHADE OF TURQUOISE ADD A SENSE OF ADVENTURE.

Left: THERE IS A DEFINITE ART TO MINING THE ORDINARY NOOKS AND CRANNIES OF A HOME. HERE, A BAY WINDOW BECOMES THE PERFECT SITE FOR A DINING SPOT. THE ASTUTE USE OF A BANQUETTE MAXIMIZES SEATING POTENTIAL, WHICH IS ENHANCED STILL FURTHER BY A CLEVERLY DESIGNED DROP-LEAF TABLE THAT CAN BE OPENED UP TO COMFORTABLY ACCOMMODATE SEVERAL MORE DINERS. CUSHIONS DECKED OUT IN PRIMARY COLORS PROVIDE BRIGHT ACCENTS FOR THE ALL-WHITE SURROUNDINGS, MAKING THIS A CHEERY SPACE IN WHICH TO DINE. **Above:** TURNING TO NOVEL SOURCES FOR DINING ROOM COMPONENTS IS ONE WAY TO COME UP WITH INTRIGUING FURNISHINGS. HERE, THE TOP OF AN OLD POOL TABLE, STRIPPED TO ITS VERY BONES, BECOMES AN EVERYDAY DINING TABLE WITH A FAR-FROM-EVERYDAY LOOK. STAINLESS STEEL CHAIRS HEIGHTEN THE TABLE'S HIGH-TECH AURA, BUT A WOOD FLOOR, SCONCES WRAPPED IN STRAW "HULA SKIRTS," AND A COLORFUL BENCH TOPPED WITH A SERAPE ADD WARMTH AND TEXTURE TO THE ROOM. AN ABSTRACT TRIANGULAR CENTERPIECE BEARS RESEMBLANCE TO A RACK OF POOL BALLS.

Opposite: AN INFORMAL DINING ROOM CAN HOST A FORMAL GATHERING WHEN DRESSED WITH THE RIGHT ACCESSORIES. HERE, A CASUAL SPACE BOASTING WROUGHT-IRON CHAIRS AND A BASIC YET QUAINT BLUE-AND-WHITE COLOR SCHEME GETS DRESSED UP WITH THE HELP OF A CHAMPAGNE BUCKET, FESTIVE CHINA, AND GOLD-RIMMED GLASSES THAT ADD JUST THE RIGHT AMOUNT OF POLISH AND FLAIR FOR AN EVENING OF ENTERTAINING.

Right, top: CASUAL DINING AREAS CAN ALSO BE GUSSIED UP WITH THE HELP OF TEXTILES, WHICH ARE HIGHLY FLEXIBLE AND AVAILABLE IN MYRIAD PATTERNS, STYLES, AND COLORS. HERE, A PLAIN UNDERSKIRT MASKS MASSIVE WOODEN LEGS, WHILE A LACY TABLECLOTH AND A PROFUSE CENTERPIECE OF DRIED FLOWERS SPRUCE UP THE SIMPLE SETTING. EVEN THE STURDY PAINTED WOODEN CHAIRS SEEM MORE ORNATE NEXT TO THE DRESSED-UP TABLE.

Right, bottom: THIS SNUG DINING AREA, CARVED OUT OF AN ENCLOSED PORCH, THINKS BIG BUT IS ACTUALLY RELATIVELY SMALL. THANKS TO A COUCHLIKE BANQUETTE, SEVERAL DINERS CAN SIT ALONG THE FAR SIDE OF THE TABLE AND ENJOY THE SAME KIND OF COMFORT AS THEIR COMPANIONS RELAXING IN OVERSIZE, CUSHIONED WICKER CHAIRS. THE BANQUETTE ALLOWS THE DINING AREA TO APPROPRIATE LESS FLOOR SPACE YET STILL LOOK ROOMY.

Opposite: SLAT-STYLE PINE PANELS SEEM
SO FAMILIAR AND ALL-AMERICAN THAT THEY AL-
MOST LULL ONE INTO OVERLOOKING THE EC-
CENTRICITIES OF THIS ENTICING DINING AREA:
THE GILDED CHANDELIER IS COUPLED WITH
GOTHICLIKE LANTERNS; AN UNUSUALLY LARGE
MOLDING TOPS THE WALLS AND BORDERS THE
CEILING; AND MISMATCHED CHAIRS SURROUND
THE TABLE. A COLLECTION OF FIESTAWARE, AN
OLD ADVERTISEMENT, AND A CLOCK FACE
RIMMED IN BLUE NEON COMBINE TO CREATE
AN INTERESTING ARRAY OF COLORS IN THIS
IDIOSYNCRATIC SPACE, WHICH HAS AN EN-
DEARING SENSE OF CHARM. **Right:**
INSTEAD OF GOING FOR CONTRAST IN THIS
PANELED DINING ROOM, THE DESIGNER USED
A PANOPLY OF COORDINATING WOODS TO
MAKE A DRAMATIC IMPACT. THE LOGS OF THE
ADIRONDACK-STYLE CHAIRS AND DINING TABLE
HARMONIZE READILY WITH THE SUPPORT BEAMS
OF THE HOUSE, WHILE AT THE SAME TIME PRO-
VIDE AN INTERESTING FOIL FOR THE POLISHED
PANELING. MOREOVER, THEY MIRROR THE SUR-
ROUNDING FOREST, WHICH BECOMES PART OF
THE DINING EXPERIENCE THANKS TO WIN-
DOWS LEFT ALLURINGLY BARE. A CUT STEEL FIX-
TURE HANGING OVERHEAD APPROPRIATELY
EVOKES A FOREST SCENE AND SERVES AS A
FASCINATING CONVERSATION PIECE.

Below: AN IMAGINATIVE PAINT JOB, PART SOPHISTICATED AND PART JUST PLAIN KITSCH, GIVES THE DEPRESSION-ERA PIECES IN THIS DINING ROOM A TOTALLY NEW TAKE ON LIFE. INSTEAD OF APPEARING ANTIQUATED AND QUAINT, THE ROOM NOW ENJOYS A CUTTING-EDGE, RETRO-CHIC APPEAL. **Opposite:** DESPITE A SOUTHWESTERN DEMEANOR, THIS ROOM IS ROOTED IN MISSION STYLING. THE CHAIRS, LIGHTING FIXTURE, AND PILASTER ARE PERFECT EXAMPLES OF THIS FORM AND ARE HIGHLIGHTED BY TOUCHES OF COUNTRY STYLING. NONETHELESS, THE ADIRONDACK DINING TABLE, A TRADING BLANKET, AND A COWHIDE RUG SHINE THROUGH TO STEAL THE SHOW.

Above: EMPLOYING FOLDING SLAT FURNITURE IS AN EASY AND QUICK WAY TO CREATE AN INFORMAL DINING SPOT ANYWHERE IN A HOME. HERE, BRIGHT HUES ADD AN ELEMENT OF SURPRISE TO THE CONVENTIONAL PIECES, TURNING THEM FROM ROUTINE TO STYLISH, WHILE BOLD TEXTILES ON THE TABLE AND A CHECKERED SISAL RUG BELOW ENHANCE THE FRESH-LOOKING APPEAL OF THE SPACE.

Below: AS DEMONSTRATED BY THE USE OF YELLOW AND GREEN IN THIS ARTS AND CRAFTS–STYLE DINING AREA, USING COLOR IS ONE WAY TO ADD INDIVIDUALITY AND WARMTH TO A ROOM WITHOUT ADDING CLUTTER. THE PALE YELLOW IS WELCOMING AND SOFTENS THE SPARE, RECTILINEAR QUALITY OF THE ARCHITECTURE AND ANTIQUE ACACIA DINING TABLE. AT THE SAME TIME, THE COOL DARK GREEN EMPHASIZES THE INTERESTING SHAPES OF THE WINDOW AND DOOR PANES, PROVIDING AN EFFECT THAT IS DISTINCTIVE, UNIQUE, AND HARMONIOUS.

Left: THANKS TO A NOVEL DINING SET THAT COUPLES QUEEN ANNE STYLING WITH BIEDERMEIER STAINS, THIS DINING ROOM IS LOADED WITH CHARACTER. RELAXED WICKER CHAIRS PUNCTUATED WITH BOLDLY PATTERNED PILLOWS CREATE THE SENSATION OF DINING AT A CARIBBEAN RESORT. **Above:** FROM THE BEAMED CEILING TO THE PRIMITIVE MANTEL TO THE PLANKED FLOOR, THIS COUNTRY COTTAGE DINING AREA EMPLOYS A WIDE RANGE OF WOODS. WARM YELLOW WALLS HELP TIE THE SPACE TOGETHER, OFFERING A FLATTERING BACK-DROP FOR THE VARIOUS WOODS AS WELL AS FOR A COLLECTION OF CHINA THAT PICKS UP THE COLORS OF THE TILED FIREPLACE. PAINTED LINES ABOVE THE MANTEL CREATE THE ILLUSION OF PANELS, WHICH APPEAR TO FRAME SMALL GROUPINGS OF THE CHINA.

COMBINED DINING

Some say that the formal dining room is on the way out, and that its demise can be traced directly to the rise of the eat-in kitchen. Although there may be some truth to this assessment, it certainly does not tell the whole story. Space constraints in general, coupled with contemporary styles of design, have led to the rise of combined dining spaces. An apartment or loft is far less likely to have its own formal dining room. But the home that has a spectacular eat-in kitchen probably also sports a stunning dining room. Formal dining rooms are not necessarily on the way out, but combined dining spaces are definitely "in."

Rooms devoted solely to dining were a luxury when they were first developed in the seventeenth century and are a luxury once again today for those of us who live in

smaller quarters. But this quandary forces us to think creatively. Dining rooms have been combined with living rooms, libraries, family rooms, kitchens, and even game rooms. And these rooms are not necessarily less formal; they are merely resourceful uses of space.

The best combined dining spaces require careful planning in order to work. It is helpful if kitchens close off or have some structural device to signal separation from the eating area, especially since they tend to get messy. And libraries should have ample storage so the space can be quickly converted back and forth. If papers are strewn across a dining table, it is less likely to be used for eating. Despite the fact that a space serves two functions, one should not encroach upon the other.

Opposite: FLAT SLAT PANELING GETS CHARACTER AND PANACHE WITH TOUCHES OF NEOCLASSICAL STYLING. DROPPED CORNICE MOLDINGS AND SHALLOW ARCHES TRIM THE PANELING, WHILE DORIC COLUMNS PAINTED GLOSSY BLACK DELINEATE THE DINING AREA. THE SAME LUSTROUS CONTRAST IS SKILLFULLY INTEGRATED INTO THE REST OF THE SPACE VIA THE WINDOW CASEMENTS.

Above: THE NARROW PASSAGE CONNECTING A KITCHEN AND DINING AREA WAS RESOURCEFULLY TURNED INTO A MINI LIBRARY WITH THE SIMPLE ADDITION OF A STOCKED BOOKSHELF. COMBINED WITH A "CHALKBOARD" PRINT AND BASIC WOODEN FURNISHINGS, THE BOOKS GIVE THE DINING AREA A SCHOOLROOM FEELING.

Left: A DINING AREA WAS CREATED IN THE MIDST OF THIS INDUSTRIAL-STYLE KITCHEN WITH THE INTRODUCTION OF A MASSIVE TABLE THAT MAINTAINS THE ORIGINAL TONE OF THE ROOM WITH ITS LUSTROUS STEEL AND MARBLE. A SUBTLE GRAY PALETTE AND A STRIKING ANGLED LAYOUT ADD STYLE AND GRACE TO THE SETTING.

Opposite: IN THIS VAST GREAT ROOM, A SOARING TWO-STORY SPACE DEFINES THE DINING AREA'S BOUNDARIES, REINFORCED BY A BUILT-IN UNIT THAT CLEVERLY INCORPORATES SEATING FOR THE LIVING ROOM AND STORAGE FOR THE DINING ROOM. ANTIQUES ARE EQUALLY AT HOME WITH CONTEMPORARY PIECES SINCE MOST OF THE FURNISHINGS ARE BASIC AND THE WALLS ARE PURE WHITE. THUS, A QUEEN ANNE DINING SET RESTS EASY NEXT TO THE SLEEK CONTEMPORARY CABINET-CUM-SOFA, WHILE AN INTRICATE VICTORIAN QUILT OFFERS A DAZZLING DISPLAY OF COLOR OVERHEAD.

Right: A MULTIFUNCTIONAL CONTEMPORARY MILIEU CAN STILL HAVE A THOROUGHLY TRADITIONAL APPEAL. IN THIS SETTING, THE DINING ROOM FEATURES A TABLE OF INTRICATE INLAID WOOD FLANKED WITH UPHOLSTERED AND SKIRTED CHAIRS; THE LIVING ROOM IS FURNISHED WITH AN OVERSTUFFED SOFA, ARMCHAIR, AND OTTOMAN; AND THE KITCHEN IS BORDERED BY A NEOCLASSICAL PILASTER AND A SUMPTUOUS MARBLE COUNTERTOP. THANKS TO THE FURNISHINGS, A SENSE OF CONVENTION AND HERITAGE IS PERVASIVE, DESPITE THE CONTEMPORARY OPENNESS OF THE SPACE.

Above: AN OPEN FLOOR PLAN CAN STILL SUPPORT A FORMAL DINING ROOM, AS EVIDENCED BY THIS LOFTLIKE SETTING. WHILE YELLOW AND BLUE UPHOLSTERY GIVES A PLAYFUL LOOK TO THE LIVING AREAS OF THE SPACE, BLACK IMBUES THE DINING AREA WITH AN ELEVATED SENSE OF DECORUM. THE PRECISE LINES OF THE DINING ROOM'S FURNISHINGS PLAY OFF THE SPACE'S AUSTERE ARCHITECTURAL ELEMENTS, INCLUDING THE STARK BLACK SUPPORT BEAMS AND BUILT-IN MINIMALIST SIDEBOARD.

Left: IN THIS CONTEMPORARY LOFT, COLOR BECOMES THE DIVIDER, WITH AN INTENSE SHADE OF TURQUOISE SETTING OFF THE PARTS OF THE SPACE THAT REVOLVE AROUND EATING. THE KITCHEN COUNTER, THE DINING CHAIRS, AND THE WALL ADJACENT TO THE TABLE ARE COVERED WITH THIS HUE, GIVING THESE AREAS AN ENTIRELY DIFFERENT AMBIENCE THAN THE LIVING ROOM BORDERED IN COOL SHADES OF SILVER AND WHITE. THE MELLOW TONES OF THE WOOD SEEN IN THE COLUMNS, TABLE, AND EXPOSED CEILING JOISTS BRING A SOFT GLOW TO THE EATING SPACE.

Opposite: Unobtrusive panel doors allow this pristine dining area to be either formal or relaxed in tone. When the doors are open, the eclectic furnishings and two-tone carpeting of the living area influence the demeanor of the dining room, creating a more casual ambience. But with the doors closed, the dining area takes on a whole different personality. In either case, ultracontemporary pieces paired together as a dining set, regal purple drapes, a polished hardwood floor, and a formal arrangement of artwork that evokes classical symmetry and styling give the dining space a refined air.

Above: In a serene setting with plush Art Deco chairs and an American Empire dining set, color is used to enhance the formality of the two activity centers. Although the carpeting throughout is a mellow beige, the dining area is set apart from the living room by the dark tones of its furnishings, which provide dynamic contrast.

Left: AUSTERE PIECES THAT ARE CLASSICS OF MODERN DESIGN DOMINATE THIS COMBINATION LIVING AND DINING ROOM, BUT THE SPACE RETAINS REMARKABLE WARMTH THANKS TO A DIVERSE MIX OF MATERIALS. ORIENTAL CARPETS AND A TRADING BLANKET ARE RADIANT IN DEEP RED WOOL AND WORK WONDERFULLY WITH THE BACKDROP OF ROUGHLY HEWN BRICK. EARTHY WOOD TOUCHES PUNCTUATE THE MIX, AND A COLLECTION OF RICE-PAPER AND PARCHMENT LAMPS CASTS A MELLOW GLOW OVER THE MILIEU. THUS, THE ROOM IS COZY, COMFORTABLE, AND CONTEMPORARY ALL AT THE SAME TIME.

Above: A WOODEN UNIT CONSISTING OF A WORK SURFACE, SHELVES, CABINETS, AND DRAWERS IS BANKED ALONG THE FAR WALL OF THIS ROOM, ALLOWING THE SPACE TO SERVE AS BOTH A DINING ROOM AND A STUDY. STREAMLINED BENEATH A VAST WINDOW, THE WORK SPACE RESTS UNOBTRUSIVELY ALONGSIDE THE DINING AREA, FOR THE OUTDOOR VIEW DRAWS THE DINER'S EYE BEYOND THE UNIT. THE DESK CHAIR, WHICH IS REALLY PART OF THE DINING SET, CAN TRAVEL FREELY BETWEEN THE TWO AREAS TO PERFORM ITS SERVICE WHERE IT IS NEEDED MOST.

Opposite: IT IS SENSIBLE TO MAKE AN EATING SPACE FLEXIBLE, AS IN THIS CONSUMMATE KITCHEN-CUM-DINING ROOM. THE KITCHEN ISLAND AND DINING ROOM TABLE, WHICH ARE MADE OF THE SAME SUMPTUOUS MATERIALS (NAMELY GRANITE AND STAINLESS STEEL), CAN BE LEFT TO PRACTICALLY BLEND INTO EACH OTHER OR CAN BE SEPARATED BY SLIDING WOODEN PANELS THAT CLOSE OFF EACH ROOM AND GIVE THE DINING AREA A MORE FORMAL CHARACTER. THE SAME AMBER WOOD VENEERS COVER THE CABINETS IN BOTH AREAS TO UNIFY THE SPACE. **Above, left:** SHINING SURFACES AND FORCEFUL SHAPES MAKE AN AWKWARD SETUP ELEGANT IN THIS KITCHEN AND DINING AREA. A STAIRWAY THAT BISECTS THE SPACE COULD HAVE BEEN A LIABILITY, BUT IN GLOSSY BLACK METAL TOPPED WITH HIGHLY POLISHED WOOD, IT IS A STUNNING SCULPTURAL FOCAL POINT THAT ALSO MANAGES TO GIVE EACH SEPARATE AREA A SENSE OF DEFINITION. A GLEAMING GLASS TABLE, SILVERY WALLS, AND SHINING STEEL SURFACES IN THE KITCHEN ALL PLAY OFF ONE ANOTHER, WHILE CREAMY AND CURVY MOLDED CHAIRS SOFTEN THE SPACE. **Above, right:** SHROUDED IN WHITE, VARIOUS MATERIALS SUCH AS WOOD SLATS, CERAMIC TILES, AND FORMICA COUNTERTOPS SEEM UNIFIED IN THIS INTRICATE, MULTILEVEL KITCHEN. MEANWHILE, WOOD FURNISHINGS IN DIFFERENT TONES SET OFF THE DINING AREA, SUPPLYING IT WITH ITS OWN IDENTITY. ALTHOUGH THE DECORATIVE ELEMENTS OF THIS SUPERBLY DESIGNED SPACE RUN THE GAMUT FROM CONTEMPORARY TO COUNTRY, THEY ALL FIT TOGETHER LIKE THE PIECES OF A COMPLEX JIGSAW PUZZLE.

Below: THIS IS TRULY A ROOM DESIGNED FOR ENTERTAINING. AFTER ENJOYING A SAVORY MEAL AND SCINTILLATING CONVERSATION AT THE DINNER TABLE, RESIDENTS AND GUESTS ALIKE CAN SLIP OVER TO THE POOL TABLE FOR MORE FUN. EVEN THE DECOR ITSELF, WITH ITS ECLECTIC BLEND OF BOLDLY PAINTED WALLS, EARTHY BASKETS, ETHNIC ARTWORKS, ITALIAN POTTERY, AND PROVINCIAL FURNITURE, IS A SOURCE OF ENTERTAINMENT, PROVIDING A FASCINATING VISUAL DIVERSION AND SPARKING CONVERSATION.

Above: COUNTRY KITSCH REIGNS SUPREME IN THIS EAT-IN-KITCHEN, WHICH WOULD PROBABLY BE QUITE ORDINARY SANS THE COLORFUL PAINT JOB. COLONIAL CABINETS HAVE BEEN PRETTIED UP WITH SUNFLOWERS AGAINST A VIBRANT TEAL BLUE, WHILE THE WOOD FLOOR HAS BEEN DECKED OUT WITH A BUSY STENCILED DESIGN IN COMPLEMENTARY HUES. A PRACTICALLY INVISIBLE GLASS TABLE WAS CHOSEN AS THE DINING SURFACE SO AS NOT TO DETRACT FROM THE BOISTEROUS PLACE SETTINGS AND THE WHIMSICAL CHAIRS, WHICH ARE TAKEOFFS ON CLASSIC COUNTRY HITCHCOCKS.

Above: ATTRACTIVE TILING SPORTING A FLORAL BORDER AND CENTRAL FLORAL DESIGN NOT ONLY MAKES A BEAUTIFUL BACKDROP IN THIS EAT-IN KITCHEN, BUT IT ALSO TRICKS THE EYE. AT FIRST GLANCE, THE RIGHT WALL LOOKS LIKE A MASSIVE BREAKFRONT, THANKS TO A MASTERFUL ARRANGEMENT OF TILES AND METICULOUSLY ARTICULATED CABINETS; IN ACTUALITY, THOUGH, THE SETUP MERELY CONSISTS OF A KITCHEN COUNTER COUPLED WITH BUILT-INS. THE TILES ALSO PROVIDE ACCENTS OF GREEN THAT COORDINATE WITH THE WICKER CHAIRS AND DOOR TRIM, ADDING WELCOME DEPTH TO THE ALMOST ENTIRELY YELLOW SURROUNDINGS.

EATING ALFRESCO

There is nothing like fresh air for stimulating an appetite, or the beauty of a dazzling landscape for setting a scene. Savoring the wonders of nature and a marvelous repast simultaneously enhances the art of dining and lends a sense of adventure to a meal. And since dining alfresco is not recognized as part of the usual routine, it is often viewed as a special event or treat.

Interestingly enough, the great outdoors actually preceded the dining room as a formal place to hold a repast. Since most homes were very small and did not have rooms devoted solely to dining, outdoor areas were reserved for more formal meals. When feasts were prepared for special occasions, they were staged in a deco-rous fashion outside. In fact, picnics were derived from the lavish banquets held outdoors during the sixteenth century, becoming less formal over time to the point where they lost their tables and chairs.

Today, eating outdoors remains a staged event, though not necessarily a formal affair. While some outdoor dining areas are temporary setups, such as a simple table and chairs in a grassy clearing, others are more permanent, consisting of pieces that remain on a patio or balcony year-round. In any case, the furnishings can be dressed up or down to accommodate meals of different levels of decorum. Although an outdoor setting is usually remarkable to begin with, the actual trappings have great power to enhance the dining experience.

Opposite: INSTEAD OF THE AIRY, PASTORAL FEELING IMPARTED BY SIMILAR PIECES COATED IN WHITE, THIS BLACK PATIO SET GIVES OFF AN AIR OF SLICK URBAN SOPHIS-TICATION. PERHAPS THE MOST STRIKING ELEMENT OF THE DECOR IS THE CHANDELIER, WHICH, WITH ITS UNUSUAL BLACK CANDLES, IS POSITIVELY BEWITCHING.

Above: IN THE MIDST OF A HEAVILY WOODED LOT, AN IMPECCABLY GROOMED WHITEWASHED PORCH MAKES A GREAT PLACE TO EAT. FILLING IT WITH THESE ADIRONDACK-STYLE TWIG FURNISHINGS IS LIKE A DOUBLE ENTENDRE: THE KNOTTY LINES OF THE PIECES PLAY OFF THE GNARLED TREES TO MAKE THE POLISHED PORCH SEEM RUSTIC, WHILE PRISTINE WHITE CUSHIONS EMBELLISHED WITH IVY CAUSE THE PENDULUM TO SWING BACK THE OTHER WAY BY ADDING A TOUCH OF REFINEMENT.

Left: A CITYSCAPE CAN BE JUST AS APPEALING AS A GORGEOUS GARDEN, ESPECIALLY IF THE SCENE IS AS CHARMING AS THE ONE OFFERED BY THESE BEAUX ARTS BUILDINGS. A TINY LITTLE TABLE FOR TWO, WHICH IS CUTE BUT CERTAINLY NOT NOTABLE ON ITS OWN, BECOMES OVERWHELMINGLY ROMANTIC AND WINSOME WEDGED INTO THIS NARROW ROOFTOP BALCONY. A BLUE-AND-WHITE CHECKED TABLECLOTH CONTRIBUTES TO THE QUAINT LOOK.

Opposite: DESPITE THE POLISH AND GRANDEUR OF THIS COURTYARD, A MODEST METAL TABLE-AND-CHAIR SET FITS RIGHT IN. THE DELICATE, CURVING LINES OF THE CHAIRS SOFTEN THE AUSTERITY OF THE METAL, WHILE A FULL-LENGTH COVERING WRAPS THE TABLE IN ELEGANCE. WITH ITS SWIRLING VINE MOTIF, THE TABLECLOTH ECHOES THE GRACEFUL LINES OF THE CHAIRS, GIVING THE ENTIRE SETUP A SENSE OF HARMONY.

Right: THIS SPACIOUS VERANDA HAS BEEN INGENIOUSLY TRANSFORMED INTO AN ARRESTING OUTDOOR DINING ROOM WITH THE HELP OF EYE-CATCHING TEXTILES. BOLD BLACK-AND-WHITE STRIPED PIECES OF FABRIC ARE SUSPENDED BETWEEN THE COLUMNS TO BECOME DAZZLING "WALLS" THAT SUPPLY PRIVACY AS WELL AS SHELTER FROM THE ELEMENTS. MOREOVER, THESE DARING TEXTILES OFFER A HUGE DOSE OF GLAMOUR TO THE SETUP.

Left: Conventions seem to dissolve when we blend the great outdoors with dining. Forget the usual trappings of formality; here, tropical foliage fills in for walls, and a thatched overhang supplants the ceiling. The "proper" Regency furnishings seem fanciful instead of stiff, and the icy marble floor looks like a refreshing oasis.

Above: A spectacular veranda, rife with such arresting architectural details as soaring columns and an artfully trussed ceiling, is a perfect place to dine. Painted white, it is like a blank slate that can take on any look depending upon how it is accessorized. In this case, simple canvas slipcovers in white give the stately setting a pure, relaxed look. Slipcovers are not only an effective means of hiding undesirable upholstery and unifying mismatched pieces, they are, above all else, an inexpensive way to achieve an exquisite look.

Opposite: THE NOVEL BACKS OF THE CHAIRS IN THIS DINING ROOM DEFTLY ECHO THE PICKET FENCE OUTSIDE, WHICH SQUARES OFF A TINY GARDEN. WHEN THE FRENCH DOORS ARE OPEN, THE TWO AREAS BECOME ONE, OWING TO THE EARTHY MATERIALS USED TO PAVE BOTH AS WELL AS THE HARMONIOUS PAIRING OF GOLDEN WOOD FURNISHINGS WITH THE BRICK PATIO. **Below:** IT IS POSSIBLE TO CAPITALIZE ON ANY GORGEOUS OPEN-AIR NOOK FOR ALFRESCO DINING. HERE, A CHARMING LITTLE CORNER OF A PORCH MAKES A PERFECT SPOT FOR EATING OUTDOORS. FURNISHED WITH AN EASY CHAIR, A ROCKER, AND A LOW-SLUNG CHECKERBOARD TABLE, THE SETTING IS IDEAL FOR A RELAXED LUNCH OR SNACK. AN ABUNDANCE OF GREENERY GIVES THE SPACE AN AIR OF SECLUSION.

Above: THANKS TO FRENCH DOORS, WHICH CAN BE FLUNG OPEN TO LET THE GLORIES BEYOND STREAM IN, IT IS POSSIBLE TO ENJOY THE PLEASURES OF DINING ALFRESCO INDOORS. HERE, WHIMSICAL FURNISHINGS COMPLEMENT AN EQUALLY FANCIFUL GARDEN. DELICATE VICTORIAN-STYLE WIRE CHAIRS THAT LOOK LIKE THEY CAME OUT OF AN ICE CREAM PARLOR ARE THE PERFECT COUNTERPOINTS TO A SUBSTANTIAL, BUT EQUALLY ORNATE, MARBLE-TOPPED TABLE. OUTSIDE, A TINY PATIO TABLE MADE OUT OF SIMILAR MATERIALS SUBTLY TIES THE TWO SPACES TOGETHER.

Above: COLUMNS ARE PERENNIAL CATALYSTS, CAPABLE OF WORKING MAGIC ON THE HUMBLEST FURNISHINGS AND RAISING THEM TO HIGHER LEVELS. HERE, THESE MAJESTIC ARCHITECTURAL ELEMENTS TRANSFORM A STRAIGHTFORWARD STONE PATIO, MODESTLY APPOINTED WITH A CEDAR SLAT TABLE AND BENCH, DIRECTOR'S CHAIRS, AND A CANVAS UMBRELLA, INTO A HIGHLY REFINED MILIEU. AND SIMPLE FOLIAGE, WHICH BECOMES LUSH USED EN MASSE, SOFTENS THE HARD-EDGED LINES OF THE PIECES, ADDING TO THE SETTING'S LUXURIOUS TONE. **Opposite:** POOLSIDE DINING IN THIS CAPTIVATING SPOT IS AN UPLIFTING AFFAIR, THANKS TO BRIGHTLY COLORED CUSHIONS THAT SERVE AS ENERGIZING ACCENTS AGAINST THE TERRA-COTTA BACKGROUND. THE BEAUTY OF THE POOL DOES THE REST, IMBUING THE SETTING WITH SERENITY.

Left: SENSIBLE CEDAR FURNITURE THAT CAN BE LEFT OUT ALL YEAR LONG IS A GREAT CHOICE FOR A SOLID BRICK PATIO. TOGETHER, THE CEDAR AND BRICK EXUDE STRENGTH AND SUBSTANCE AS THEY STAND UP TO THE ELEMENTS. POTTED ANNUALS IN VIVID COLORS LIVEN UP THE EARTHY HUES, WHILE A VIVID FLORAL CLOTH GIVES THE TABLE A FESTIVE AIR.

Opposite: A MERE CLEARING, COMPLETE WITH GRAVEL AND DIRT UNDERFOOT, GOES FROM UNPRETEN- TIOUS TO ENCHANTING THANKS TO ACCESSORIES THAT DEFTLY ENHANCE THE SETTING'S NATURAL ATTRIBUTES. FOUR WHITE FOLDING CHAIRS, ACCENTED BY TWO CHAIRS THAT ARE A BIT MORE BAROQUE, MIRROR THE AIRY FEELING OF THE OUTDOORS, WHILE A PINK-AND-WHITE CHECKED TABLECLOTH ECHOES THE LOCA- TION'S NATURAL COLOR SCHEME.

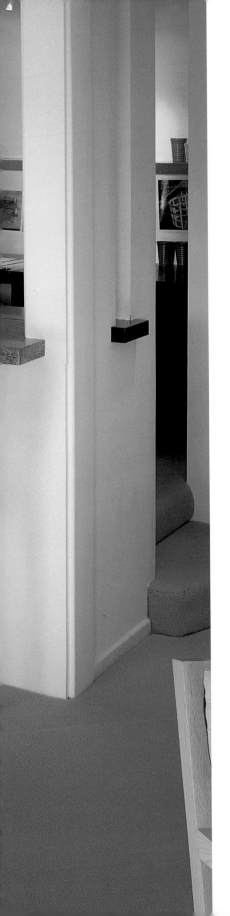

PART FOUR
HOME OFFICES

INTRODUCTION

Millions of people are going home to work, either full-time or part-time, and that number is growing every day. In the United States, the actual figure now tops forty-five million people and is expected to reach close to sixty million in just a few years, says Link Resources, a New York research firm that compiles an annual work-at-home survey. The "electronic cottagers" that Alvin Toffler envisioned back in 1980 and the "hoffices" (home/offices) that Faith Popcorn anticipated in 1989 are now upon us.

Ironically, the notion of working at home is not new. Merchants and artisans have labored out of their residences all through the ages. Not until the Industrial Revolution did this standard change, since the demand for employees to staff offices and factories drew people from their homes to central workplaces.

But just as technology revolutionized the way we lived and worked in the nineteenth century, it is doing so once again, and the base of our economy is changing from industry to information. Instead of using heavy machinery, we can work on computers, which are far more compact and mobile. And thanks to the microchip, which has made home computing easy and efficient, the hardware that holds all the data we need is significantly smaller than ever before. Further technological advances, including fax machines, modems, voice mail systems, productivity software, and electronic mail, can be used just as easily in the home as in corporate environments. An office can be placed practically anywhere today, so we have come full circle and are returning to the home.

And for good reason. Who can resist a thirty-second commute? Or wearing exactly what one wants to work? Or better yet, who can turn down the prospect of working in his or her own abode, toiling away while comfortably ensconced in a tailor-made milieu? Furniture and

Opposite: At the far end of a dramatic great room, complete with a sweeping overhang from the second story, a home office is ingeniously positioned to take advantage of the space. Natural light flows in from the room's French doors; an Oriental area rug on top of wall-to-wall carpeting sets the space apart; and the cockpitlike design of the desk, which wraps around the work area, keeps everything within easy reach and gives the space a measure of privacy.

office equipment companies are beginning to produce beautifully designed scaled-down pieces that work splendidly in home-based settings. In fact, the trend to work out of a home office is fueling a whole new market in the furniture industry—one that emphasizes pieces that can accommodate an ever-changing array of equipment and an always growing array of needs. But comfort, form, and function must converge in these pieces; workers want and need attractive furnishings that will not only transform areas of their homes into environments conducive to their particular working habits, but will also meet their aesthetic tastes.

Creating the right kind of home office is a fundamental need that every home worker must meet. Anyone can pack all sorts of sophisticated equipment into a space, but making that space efficient and effective, as well as comfortable and appealing, is truly a challenge, as is finding an appropriate

Above: SERENITY REIGNS SUPREME IN THIS TRANQUIL SETTING, THANKS TO ITS STREAMLINED DESIGN. THE ELEVATED BOOKSHELF IS AN UNUSUAL YET EFFECTIVE DEVICE THAT GIVES THE ROOM BROADER PROPORTIONS AND HELPS EVOKE AN ORIENTAL OVERTONE IN THE SPACE. GLOSSY BLACK WORK SURFACES, DARK RED WOOD VENEERS, AND COOL GRAY-PAINTED WALLS, ALONG WITH THE IMMACULATE STATE OF THE ENTIRE OFFICE SETUP, CONTRIBUTE TO THIS AURA.

space in the first place. Since the equipment available is incredibly compact, the options are seemingly endless. Closets, bookcases, and even kitchen crannies are all contenders as work spaces, and can be just as vital as a whole spare room. And issues such as seating, storage, lighting, and layout must be taken into account. Some home offices are merely attempts to duplicate a corporate setting in a spare room that is furnished with massive desks, file cabinets, and credenzas.

But more often than not, people choose to inject their home offices with personality and individual style.

Some people consult designers, while others do it on their own. In either case, the home worker's tastes and preferences are extremely important in the process of creating this sort of office, for such a work space is first and foremost a part of the home. The decor that the individual selects must ultimately be integrated into his or her abode.

Above: AN INTERESTING HOME OFFICE THAT HAS LOADS OF STYLE CAN EASILY BE CREATED WITH THE RIGHT KIND OF FURNISHINGS. HERE, PIECES THAT ARE PRIME EXAMPLES OF CONTEMPORARY DESIGN PROVIDE AN EFFECTIVE FOUNDATION FOR A REMARKABLY APPOINTED WORK SPACE. EVERYTHING ABOUT THIS DESK AND COMPACT CREDENZA POINTS TO VERSATILITY, SUCH AS FOLDOUT EXTENSIONS ON THE WORK SURFACES AND CASTERS ON THE LEGS. FURNISHINGS OF THIS ILK CAN BE USED IN ANY SETTING TO CARVE OUT AN EXCEPTIONAL WORK ENVIRONMENT IN A SMALL AMOUNT OF SPACE.

FASHIONED FOR FUNCTION

Most home offices start out very different from the way they end up. A simple desk with a phone and computer may be all that is needed to get going. Then, perhaps, a printer and photocopier are added to the ensemble. Before long, files crowd the floor and supplies consume the space in a slapdash fashion.

Offices need to be highly functional domains, so a lot of thought must be given to the way the space is used and what it contains. While a bare-bones setup may serve the needs of some, a full-service spread, complete with a conference table and a work space for a coworker, may be necessary for others. But whether one employs a decorative desk or a sensible work station, the place in which work is conducted needs to be efficiently

configured so that resources are kept within easy reach. Putting a file cabinet or printer at the opposite end of the room from the desk does not make sense if these pieces of equipment are used frequently.

Built-ins are one of the best ways to tailor a work space to individual needs. They are capable of everything from housing electronic equipment to storing important files to saturating a space with convenient out-of-the-way shelves. Fabricated in many materials and fashioned in dozens of different decorative styles, built-ins can be easily incorporated into any milieu. A sleek and contemporary unit may be elegant in a laminate, while a traditional-looking setup can be downright luxurious in wood.

Opposite: WITH THE HELP OF A FEW MODEST MATERIALS (SUCH AS FORMICA WORK SURFACES, PREFABRICATED WALL-HUNG SHELVES, AND FILE CABINETS) AND AN ASTUTE USE OF SPACE, THIS OFFICE WAS DESIGNED FOR BOTH APPEARANCE AND PERFORMANCE. THE MONOCHROMATIC APPROACH GIVES THE UNIT AN EXPENSIVELY ELEGANT LOOK, WHILE A FEW SIMPLE ACCESSORIES, SUCH AS WICKER CHAIRS, A WARM RED RUG, AND SOME KNICKKNACKS IN EARTHY TONES, ADD POLISH TO THE ROOM. **Above:** A CREATIVE APPROACH BEGOT THIS ASYMMETRICAL WALL UNIT, WHICH EFFECTIVELY ORGANIZES ITS OWNER. ODDLY SHAPED ITEMS SUCH AS ENVELOPES, CANCELED CHECKS, AND EVEN MASSIVE PHONE BOOKS ALL HAVE THEIR OWN SPECIAL SPOTS. BEST OF ALL, THIS SETUP REQUIRES A MINIMAL AMOUNT OF SPACE AND CAN WORK IN A VARIETY OF DIFFERENT SETTINGS.

Above: WRAPAROUND BUILT-INS RIMMING THE PERIMETER OF THIS ROOM MAKE THE SPACE SEEM LARGER THAN IT ACTUALLY IS. THE SIMPLE YET REFINED LIGHT-TONED COLOR SCHEME FURTHER OPENS UP THE ROOM, WHICH COMFORTABLY ACCOMMODATES TWO SPACIOUS WORK STATIONS. FRENCH DOORS ADD TO THE AIRY FEELING, USHERING IN LIGHT FROM A SOURCE OTHER THAN THE OFFICE'S SINGLE WINDOW. **Opposite:** HERE, A LARGE OPEN ROOM HAS BEEN PARTITIONED BY A STRIKING SYSTEM OF SHELVES. AS A RESULT, AN INTIMATE WORK SPACE WITH AN EFFICIENT GALLEY-STYLE LAYOUT HAS BEEN CREATED. THE DYNAMIC SHADE OF YELLOW THAT LINES THE SHELVES ENERGIZES THE AREA, PREVENTING IT FROM APPEARING TOO STERILE.

Opposite: FRONTED WITH LUXURIOUS WOOD VENEERS, THIS UNIT IS SET OFF FROM THE REST OF THE WHITE ROOM AND THEREBY IMBUED WITH AN AIR OF IMPORTANCE. OVERHEAD CABINETS PROVIDE EXTRA STORAGE THAT CAN BE USED FOR EITHER WORK-RELATED RECORDS OR PERSONAL EFFECTS, SUCH AS OUT-OF-SEASON CLOTHING. **Below:** JUST OVER TWO FEET (60CM) DEEP, THIS SPACE WAS CHOPPED OFF A HALLWAY AND TURNED INTO AN OFFICE WITH THE HELP OF A SIMPLE DARK GLASS PARTITION. THE UTILITARIAN CORK-COVERED WALL AND IMAGINATIVE STEPPED-UP WOODEN WORK SURFACE ARE AT THE SAME TIME EXTREMELY BASIC AND INVENTIVELY BOLD, ALLOWING THE MINUTE SETUP TO MAKE A MAJOR IMPACT.

Above: GIVEN THE SPACIOUS NATURE OF TODAY'S WALK-IN CLOSETS, THE DECISION TO CONVERT ONE INTO A HOME OFFICE MAKES A LOT OF SENSE. HERE, A FAIRLY AMPLE CLOSET HAS BEEN COMPLETELY REDONE FOR AN ARCHITECT, WITH SHELVING AND WORK STATIONS TAKING THE PLACE OF CLOTHING RODS. SHIFTING BETWEEN THE DRAFTING TABLE AND THE COMPUTER IS BOTH COMFORTABLE AND QUICK WITH THE HELP OF A CHAIR ON WHEELS, AND SLIDING PARTITIONS ARE OUTFITTED WITH TRANSLUCENT GLASS SO THAT THEY CONTINUE TO ALLOW LIGHT INTO THE SPACE WHEN THE DOORS ARE CLOSED, WHILE AT THE SAME TIME PRESERVING A DEGREE OF PRIVACY.

Below: BUILT-INS CAN BE SLEEK, HIGHLY STYLED, AND SOPHISTICATED WITHOUT BEING SPECIFICALLY CONTEMPORARY. ELEMENTS OF COLONIAL STYLING AND THE WARM BURNISHED HUE OF WOOD GIVE THIS ROOM A COUNTRY DEMEANOR, EVEN THOUGH IT INCORPORATES THOROUGHLY UP-TO-DATE DETAILS SUCH AS FORMICA COUNTERTOPS. THE WINDSOR ROCKERS AND CHAIR REINFORCE THE ROOM'S PERIOD DECOR. **Opposite:** IT TOOK NOTHING MORE THAN A FEW PLANKS OF WOOD TO FABRICATE THIS SIMPLE OFFICE, BUT THE EFFECT IS STRIKING THANKS TO THE EXCEPTIONAL BEAUTY OF THE SETTING. THE VIEW MAKES A MAGNIFICENT BACKDROP; THE LOCATION OFFERS AN ABUNDANCE OF NATURAL LIGHT; AND THE MINIMAL—BUT EFFECTIVE—SETUP ALLOWS THE SPECTACULAR ARCHITECTURAL DETAILING OF THE STRUCTURE TO SHINE THROUGH. THE OFFICE'S RICH WOOD BLENDS IN SPLENDIDLY WITH THE WOODSY OUTDOOR SURROUNDINGS THAT ARE SO PREVALENT THANKS TO THE IMMENSE WINDOWS.

Above: THIS BUILT-IN UNIT HAS BEEN ARTFULLY CONSTRUCTED TO HOLD A WIDE VARIETY OF OFFICE NECESSITIES. IT NOT ONLY INCORPORATES A CABINET THAT STORES LEGAL-SIZE HANGING FILES AND A COMPUTER DRIVE INVENTIVELY PLACED VERTICALLY, BUT IT ALSO MAKES THE MOST OF A SHALLOW ALCOVE THAT WAS FORMERLY A CLOSET. NOW A BOOKCASE, THIS NOOK HAS A GLASSED-IN TOP THAT KEEPS BOOKS DUST-FREE, WHILE THE OPEN BOTTOM LEAVES THE OCCUPANT A LITTLE EXTRA LEG ROOM.

Opposite: IN THIS FAMILY ROOM, A SET OF BUILT-IN SHELVES HAS BEEN REVAMPED WITH THE SIMPLE ADDITION OF A FILE CABINET, A CHAIR, AND SOME WOODEN PLANKS. THE PALE OFF-WHITE HUE OF THE WALLS AND THE LIGHT SHADE OF WOOD SET THE PERFECT TONE FOR THE ROOM, WHICH OPENS OUT ONTO A REFRESHING TERRACE WITH A BREATHTAKING VIEW OF THE OCEAN. THE USE OF A BEIGE WICKER WASTEPAPER BASKET, WHICH FURTHER COMPLEMENTS THE ROOM'S AIRY TONE, SHOWS HOW EVEN THE SMALLEST OFFICE ACCOUTREMENTS CAN BE INCORPORATED TO COORDINATE WITH THE OVERALL DECOR. **Below:** EVEN THOUGH THIS BALCONY OFF A STAIRWELL IS A PUBLIC AREA OF THE HOME, IT EFFECTIVELY HOUSES A PRODUCTIVE HOME OFFICE. FACING AWAY FROM THE CONVERSATIONAL SEATING AREA, THE ACTUAL WORK SPACE IS SITUATED COMFORTABLY OUT OF RANGE OF THE SPACE'S TRAFFIC PATTERNS. THE LIGHT NATURAL WOOD USED FOR THE DESK AREA, ALONG WITH THE DEEP GREEN HUE OF THE SURROUNDING WALL, VISUALLY DISTINGUISHES THE WORK SPACE FROM THE REST OF THE WHITE BALCONY. UNLIKE THE SEATING AREA, WHICH IS ILLUMINATED BY SOOTHING SOFT WHITE LIGHT, THE DESK AREA HAS FLUORESCENT LIGHTING, WHICH FURTHER SEPARATES THE WORK SPACE FROM THE REST OF THE ROOM.

Above: THIS RELATIVELY SPACIOUS AND ELEGANTLY NEUTRAL OFFICE WASHED IN A WARM OFF-WHITE HUE HAS BEEN CLEVERLY CARVED OUT OF A MODESTLY SIZED SPACE. WRAPPING AROUND A NARROW CORNER, THE BUILT-IN WORK SURFACE IS ABLE TO ACCOMMODATE A COMPUTER AND SEPARATE WORK STATION, WHILE A CHAIR ON WHEELS CAN BE ROLLED BETWEEN THESE TWO DESK AREAS. CAREFULLY PLANNED SHELVES MOUNTED ABOVE THE WORK SURFACE HARBOR ENOUGH NOOKS AND CRANNIES TO PLACE AN ASSORTMENT OF WORKING MATERIALS WITHIN EASY REACH.

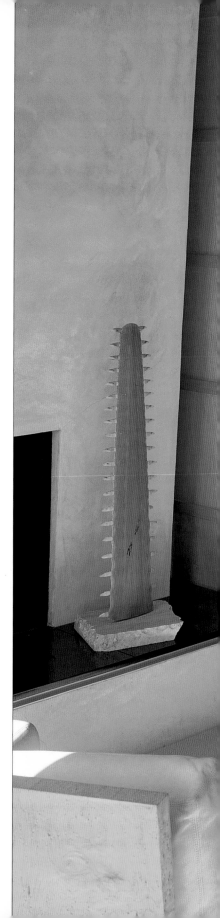

Right: THIS FORMER BAR AREA OVERLOOKING A STUNNING LIVING ROOM WAS INGENIOUSLY CONVERTED INTO A STYLISH, COMPACT HOME OFFICE. THE HANDSOME GRANITE COUNTERTOP IS JUST AS APPROPRIATE FOR WORKING AS IT IS FOR EATING AND DRINKING, AND THE AMPLE STORAGE SPACE IN THE GALLEYLIKE SETUP IS SUPPLEMENTED BY SHELVES JUST OUTSIDE ITS ENTRANCE. A WHIMSICAL LAMP AND HIGHLY STYLED STOOLS, ALL IN HUES OF BEIGE AND BLACK, SERVICE THE OFFICE AREA AND BLEND IN BEAUTIFULLY WITH THE LIVING ROOM'S WARM CONTEMPORARY FURNISHINGS.

Above: USED TO ITS FULLEST POTENTIAL, EVEN A SLIVER OF SPACE CAN BE TRANSFORMED INTO A PRODUCTIVE OFFICE. HERE A SMALL YET SLEEKLY STYLED HOME OFFICE HAS BEEN SKILLFULLY TACKED ONTO THE SCANT SPACE SURROUNDING A WINDOW. THE DESK'S ELLIPTICAL SHAPE, WHICH SOFTENS THE LOOK OF THE SETUP, EXPANDS THE DEPTH OF THE WORK SURFACE AND IS ECHOED BY TWO SHELVES THAT LEND THE UNIT AN AIR OF SOPHISTICATION. ILLUMINATION IS PROVIDED BY BOTH HIDDEN RECESSED LIGHTING AND A TASK LAMP.

Below: A TOTALLY PRIVATE SPACE HAS BEEN LITERALLY SLICED OFF ANOTHER ROOM TO CREATE THIS QUIET AND SECLUDED OFFICE, WHICH IS FULLY STOCKED WITH AUDIO-VISUAL EQUIPMENT AS WELL AS TRADITIONAL BUSINESS SUPPLIES. THE DIVIDING WALL IS INGENIOUSLY FITTED WITH AN INTERIOR WINDOW, WHICH ALLOWS ILLUMINATION TO FLOW THROUGH FROM THE AREA'S ONLY SOURCE OF NATURAL LIGHT AND CAN ALSO BE OPENED OR CLOSED FOR SOUNDPROOFING AND VENTILATION. A MIRRORED WALL IS EMPLOYED TO VISUALLY ENLARGE THE BEDROOM THAT HAS BEEN REDUCED IN SIZE ON ACCOUNT OF THE OFFICE CREATION. **Opposite:** THIS CHARMING TABLEAU UNDER A GRACEFUL STAIRCASE IS ACTUALLY AN ARTFULLY ARRANGED READING SPACE. ALTHOUGH THE CHOICE OF ACCESSORIES SEEMS PREDICATED BY FORM, THEY ARE ALL ACTUALLY QUITE FUNCTIONAL. THE ELEGANT TABLE THAT SERVES AS A DESK PROVIDES AN ADEQUATE WORK SURFACE; A SIDEBOARD ABUTTING THE PIECE HAS SEVERAL AMPLE DRAWERS FOR STORAGE; AND A FUNKY HALOGEN FIXTURE IS A SUPERIOR SOURCE OF LIGHT. PLUS, A LARGE SHELVING UNIT ADJACENT TO THE AREA OFFERS PLENTIFUL STORAGE FOR PERIODICALS.

Above: SITUATED ON A BALCONY THAT OFFERS A LOVELY VIEW OF THE DINING ROOM BELOW, THIS NOVEL HOME OFFICE PROVIDES PLENTY OF ROOM FOR SPREADING OUT PAPERS AND STORING SUPPLIES WITHOUT EATING UP MUCH OF THE HOME'S FUNCTIONAL SPACE. LIGHT FLOODS THE AREA THANKS TO AN ARRESTING SKYLIGHT AND A MATCHING GLASS-PANELED WALL, MAKING THIS OFFICE A CHEERFUL, UPLIFTING PLACE IN WHICH TO WORK. THESE PANELS ARE ECHOED BY A ROW OF GLASS BLOCKS THAT ADDS A TOUCH OF ELEGANCE AS WELL AS PREVENTS OBJECTS FROM PLUMMETING OFF THE BALCONY'S EDGE.

DOUBLE-DUTY SPACES

"A room of one's own," which the British author Virginia Woolf found to be a crucial prerequisite for creativity, is ideal for anyone working out of the home. But many of us do not have the luxury of possessing an entire room that can be devoted solely to our work.

Hence, the rise of the double-duty room: an area decidedly devoted to two or more endeavors. Although the notion of establishing a work space in a multipurpose room is definitely not new, this type of office is now being designed far more imaginatively and effectively than ever before. A good deal of deliberation is going into the process, and the spaces that are emerging reflect both practical needs and decorative tastes. Because these offices are configured in shared spaces, close attention is focused upon visually integrating the work area with the surrounding decor. Office furnishings are often innovative and informal, taking their cues from the rest of the room. Shelves are turned over to objects an occupant may enjoy looking at, and artwork enlivens the walls.

Any kind of room can be mined for a home office, from a guest room to a full-service gym. But bedrooms, family rooms, and libraries seem to be the areas that are most often adapted for this purpose, as they usually harbor the largest amount of excess space.

Opposite: WITH PROPER PLANNING, A BEDROOM CAN BECOME A COMPREHENSIVE AND EFFICIENT HOME OFFICE. THE ELEMENTS USED TO CREATE THIS ROOMY WORK AREA HAVE BEEN ASTUTELY TAILORED TO MAKE THE MOST OF THE SPACE. ROUNDED CABINETS PROVIDE EXTRA DEPTH BY ENVELOPING THE AREA'S CORNERS, WHICH WOULD OTHERWISE BE DEAD SPACE. WHILE SHELVES ABOVE THE CENTER OF THE DESK HAVE BEEN RAISED TO ACCOMMODATE A COMPUTER MONITOR, THE CORNER CABINETS DROP DOWN TO FURNISH MORE ROOM FOR STORAGE. CAREFUL ATTENTION HAS ALSO BEEN DIRECTED TOWARD THE DECOR, AS EVIDENCED BY THE CREAMY TONES OF THE OFFICE, WHICH ECHO THE BEIGE ACCENTS OF THE BED AREA. **Above:** SIMPLE ORNAMENTAL EMBELLISHMENTS ALLOW THE CLUBBY DECORATIVE THEME OF A BEDROOM TO CARRY OVER INTO THE BUILT-IN OFFICE THAT SHARES THE SPACE. THE WORK SURFACE AND DRAWERS ARE ARTICULATED WITH DETAILING REMINISCENT OF REGENCY STYLING, WHILE THE WHOLE UNIT IS PAINTED A DEEP SHADE OF GREEN. A MAJESTIC LEATHER AND WOOD CHAIR WITH A DECIDEDLY BRITISH OVERTONE COMPLETES THE LOOK AND COORDINATES WITH THE ORNATELY CARVED MAHOGANY BED.

Above: BECAUSE DEVOTING AN ENTIRE ROOM TO A HOME OFFICE CAN BE DIFFICULT, THE OWNER OF THIS FULLY EQUIPPED YET CASUAL WORK SPACE ADDED AMENITIES THAT ALLOW IT TO FUNCTION AS A GUEST ROOM AS WELL. A COMFORTABLE SLEEPING AREA, WHICH HOUSES MUCH-NEEDED BUILT-IN STORAGE, WAS CARVED OUT OF AN ALCOVE BY TOPPING A BANK OF LOW DRAWERS WITH AN INVITING MATTRESS AND THROW PILLOWS. **Right:** A CAREFULLY EDITED MILIEU DEMANDS AN OFFICE TO MATCH. IN THIS ELEGANT BUT AUSTERE BEDROOM, ATTENTION IS IMMEDIATELY DRAWN TO THE DRAMATIC ASPECTS OF THE SPACE, SUCH AS THE HIGH CONTRAST OF THE BEIGE AND BLACK COLOR SCHEME AND THE STRIKING FRANK GEHRY BENTWOOD CHAIR. AN OFFICE THAT COMPLEMENTS, RATHER THAN COMPETES WITH, THESE COMPONENTS IS UNOBTRUSIVELY POSITIONED AT THE FAR END OF THE ROOM. THE WRAPAROUND DESK, FABRICATED FROM THE SAME MATERIALS AS THE BED AND BUILT-IN CABINETS, FEATURES THE SAME KIND OF STYLING AS THESE OTHER FURNISHINGS, WHILE THE HIGH-CONTRAST MOTIF IS CARRIED THROUGH BY THE BLACK SHELVES AND DESK CHAIR.

Opposite: A warm, rich cherry wall unit, which is neutral enough to blend in with pieces from other eras, such as a Mission rocker and a Victorian clothes rack, is used to outfit this bedroom with a functional work space. The furniture's physical versatility is an added bonus: note the nightstand, which is actually a matching file cabinet.

Below: An unusual unit modeled after a traditional partners desk but altered with clever modifications allows this dressing area to double as an office. Floor-to-ceiling mirrors cover the doors to the closet, which provides storage for both clothes and office accoutrements, and visually expand the space. But a low-pile carpet and a total lack of clutter create the open and airy feeling of the area.

Above: Flanked by stately white columns, this work space is graced with a majestic, classical ambience that is refreshingly different from the casual yet busy tone of the family room sharing the area. Nonetheless, the decor retains a sense of harmony thanks to the emerald green walls that envelop the room.

Opposite: AN OFFICE TUCKED AWAY IN A CORNER OF A KITCHEN CAN STILL AFFORD AMPLE STORAGE. DESK DRAWERS AND A WHOLE WALL OF CABINETS ARE CONFIGURED TO LOOK LIKE KITCHEN CUPBOARDS, BUT ARE ACTUALLY A BIT DEEPER AND HIDE FILES AND WORKING MATERIALS. **Below:** FOLDING DOORS ARE USED TO CONCEAL THIS WELL-DESIGNED WORK SPACE THAT HAS BEEN CREATED OFF A KITCHEN DINING AREA. UNOBTRUSIVELY PROMOTING THE SEPARATION OF WORK AND FAMILY LIFE, THESE DOORS CAN BE CLOSED SO THAT THE KITCHEN RECLAIMS A MORE HOMEY AMBIENCE WHEN THE FAMILY IS GATHERED THERE FOR MEALS.

Above: EVEN THOUGH THIS HOME OFFICE IS NOTHING MORE THAN A WORK STATION AT ONE END OF A KITCHEN, IT IS SURPRISINGLY COMPREHENSIVE. A CREDENZA THAT RUNS FROM A BANK OF BUILT-IN KITCHEN EQUIPMENT TO THE ROOM'S FAR WALL IS FABRICATED FROM THE SAME MATERIALS AS THE "OFFICIAL" KITCHEN CABINETS, AND CONSISTS OF FILE CABINETS AND SUPPLY DRAWERS TOPPED BY A VAST WORK SURFACE. THE AREA RECEIVES AN ABUNDANCE OF NATURAL LIGHT FROM LARGE WINDOWS AND A SKYLIGHT, WHILE A BANK OF RECESSED CANISTERS PROVIDES TASK LIGHTING.

Opposite: DESPITE THE FACT THAT BASIC FURNISHINGS HAVE BEEN USED TO CONFIGURE THIS COMBINATION OFFICE/SITTING ROOM, COLOR AND TEXTURE IMBUE IT WITH A POLISHED AIR OF SOPHISTICATION. THE CARPETING, WALLS, BLINDS, BUILT-IN SHELVES, AND DESK ARE ALL EXECUTED IN THE SAME SUBTLE, WARM TONES, AND A RICH VELVETEEN GIVES THE SLEEPER SOFA A MEASURE OF OPULENCE. THE OVERALL EFFECT IS ANYTHING BUT ORDINARY.

Above: OPTIMAL USE IS MADE OF A CORNER IN THIS FAMILY ROOM: A DRAFTING TABLE IS SITUATED NEXT TO THE SOURCE OF NATURAL LIGHT; A DESK IS PLACED IN A RECESSED ALCOVE; AND A SET OF BUILT-IN SHELVES IS POSITIONED IN BETWEEN TO ALLOW EASY ACCESS FROM EITHER WORK STATION. WORKS OF ART INTERSPERSED IN THIS TINY AREA, WHICH IS BUT A SMALL PART OF THE ROOM, IMPART IT WITH SIGNIFICANCE AND DRAMA, WHILE A UNIQUE TWO-TONE MOLDING TREATMENT THAT RIMS THE ROOM'S PERIMETER UNIFIES THE OFFICE WITH THE REST OF THE SPACE.

Left: SITUATED AT ONE END OF A FAMILY ROOM, THIS HOME OFFICE HAS EFFECTIVELY BEEN SET APART FROM THE REST OF THE SPACE WITH THE HELP OF A WRAPAROUND WORK SURFACE—FORMED BY A STRATEGIC CONFIGURATION OF MIX-AND-MATCH PIECES—THAT ACTS AS A DIVIDER. COMFORTABLE ARMCHAIRS FACE INWARD TOWARD THE DESK, FURTHER IMBUING THE OFFICE AREA WITH INTIMACY. **Above:** THE OFFICELIKE CHORES OF EVERYDAY LIFE, SUCH AS PAYING BILLS OR WRITING LETTERS, CAN BE STREAMLINED BY HAVING A SPECIAL WORK SPACE. HERE, A CORNER OF A FORMAL LIBRARY IS DEVOTED TO THESE NECESSARY TASKS WITH THE HELP OF A FOLDING SCREEN THAT IS CLEVERLY USED TO DISPLAY INCOMING CORRESPONDENCE AND IMPORTANT REMINDERS. WHILE THESE NOTES REMAIN NEATLY OUT OF SIGHT FROM OTHER VANTAGE POINTS IN THE ROOM, THEY ARE HIGHLY VISIBLE AT THE DESK. FURTHERMORE, THIS NOVEL USE OF THE SCREEN FREES UP DRAWER SPACE FOR OFFICE SUPPLIES AND DOCUMENTS OF A MORE PRIVATE NATURE.

Right: INTEGRATING A FUNCTIONAL WORKING AREA INTO AN ELEGANT MILIEU CAN OFTEN BE CHALLENGING. HERE, AN EXQUISITE MAHOGANY TABLE, WHICH PICKS UP THE WOOD OF THE FIREPLACE DIRECTLY OPPOSITE, DOUBLES AS A DESK IN A SOPHISTICATED BUT ECLECTIC LIVING ROOM. STACKS OF BOOKS INTERSPERSED IN THE SPACE CREATE A SLIGHTLY NONCHALANT MOOD.

Above: THERE IS ROOM FOR WORK AND PLAY IN THIS DEFTLY ARRANGED SPACE, WHICH SERVES AS AN OFFICE AND EXERCISE CENTER FOR A COUPLE. AN ALCOVE OFF THE ROOM'S ENTRANCE INCORPORATES A DESK, SHELVES, AND FILE CABINETS, AND IS CLEVERLY ENLARGED WITH THE ADROIT USE OF A FLOOR-TO-CEILING MIRROR AND RECESSED LIGHTING. ANOTHER DESK HEMS IN THE WORK AREA AND SEPARATES IT FROM THE GYM, CREATING AN INFORMAL BUT EFFECTIVE BARRIER THAT ENHANCES THE PERFORMANCE OF THE SPACE.

TRADITIONALLY SPEAKING

The very notion of a traditional home office conjures up images of a British men's club, replete with sumptuous paneling, soothing dark hues, and pieces upholstered in leather. But the word "traditional" embraces many different styles, all connected by the fact that they have achieved historical acceptance and renown.

Rooms that are referred to as "traditional" fill us with a certain response, for they embrace a decor that we find familiar. The furnishings are either old or made to look that way, and they remind us of days gone by. Yet despite this common thread, they come in an amazingly wide variety of incarnations.

An office brimming with neoclassical styling can be just as traditional as one that is quintessentially British club—as can a Victorian vista that is crammed with extravagant Baroque pickings. Moreover, any of these various styles can be combined yet still evoke a mood that seems true to a specific tradition.

Thus, the traditional home office of today may be filled with a combination of furnishings that are Colonial, Shaker, or Federal in form, but have an all-American historical appeal. Or pieces that are Empire, Regency, and Biedermeier in origin can be used to make a room seem decidedly European. Even styles from the late nineteenth and twentieth centuries, such as Victorian, Arts and Crafts, and Mission, as well as those derived from ethnic origins, are eligible for the mix. What matters is mood rather than strict adherence to a style's purity.

Opposite: Knotty pine paneling delineated with Federal styling imparts a sense of history to this handsome room that is the epitome of a traditional home office. A cozy sitting area overlooking an inviting fireplace makes an ideal spot for working with clients or relaxing. **Above:** Sumptuous tufted leather chairs and a dark stained wooden desk lend an air of authority to this comfortable home office. But floral-patterned drapes, an abundance of greenery, and the golden hue of the oak wainscoting and wall unit liven up the space, giving it a welcoming and reassuring feel. Prized possessions, including an antique globe and an old-fashioned typewriter, adorn the room and contribute to the traditional tone.

Opposite: THE QUINTESSENTIAL CLUB LOOK IS RELATIVELY EASY TO ACHIEVE IN AN OFFICE, EVEN ONE WITHOUT PANELING. UPHOLSTERED PIECES COVERED IN BOLD PATTERNS OR COLORS, SIMPLE TRADITIONAL FURNISHINGS FABRICATED IN DARK WOODS, AND VIVID, FLORAL AREA CARPETS OVER WOOD FLOORS ARE ALL DECORATIVE DEVICES THAT DO THE TRICK. SHELVES AND WALLS PAINTED IN STRONG, DARK HUES FURTHER IMBUE THE ROOM WITH INTENSITY. HERE, AN ELABORATE THREE-TIER CANOPIED WINDOW TREATMENT THAT IMMEDIATELY ENGAGES THE EYE ADDS EVEN MORE DRAMA AND DECORUM TO THE ROOM.

Above: ALTHOUGH THE OVERALL EFFECT OF THIS CHARMING HOME OFFICE IS "COUNTRY MANOR QUAINT," THE PIECES USED TO ACHIEVE THIS LOOK ARE ACTUALLY QUITE SOPHISTICATED AND ECLECTIC. A FRENCH ARMCHAIR MANS AN EMPIRE DESK; BIEDERMEIER FRUITWOOD CHAIRS SURROUND AN EMPIRE TABLE; AND A QUEEN ANNE WING CHAIR FLANKS SHELVES LADEN WITH BOOKS. THESE FURNISHINGS PROVIDE SPECIFIC AREAS FOR WORKING, MEETING, AND READING, WHILE DECORATIVE TOUCHES, INCLUDING FLORAL DRAPES, BEAUTIFUL TEAL WALLS, ORIENTAL CARPETS, AND A RUSTIC COFFERED CEILING, LULL ONE INTO SEEING THE SPACE IN A FAR MORE CASUAL LIGHT.

Above: THIS VARIATION ON THE CLUB THEME FOLLOWS ALL THE RULES, WITH THE EXCEPTION OF ITS INTERESTING WALL TREATMENT. ALTHOUGH PANELING IS USED ON THE BUILT-IN SHELVES AND ON MOST OF THE WALLS, THE AREA SANDWICHED BETWEEN THE MOLDING AND CEILING IS FINISHED OFF WITH PATTERNED WALLPAPER DISPLAYING DEEP SHADES OF BLUE AND RED THAT COORDINATE WITH THE UPHOLSTERED ARMCHAIR, THE AREA RUG, AND EVEN THE LAMP SHADES. TO GIVE THE ROOM ADDED DEPTH, THE CEILING HAS BEEN PAINTED A SOFT SHADE OF BROWN THAT IS SUBSTANTIALLY LIGHTER THAN THE OTHER COLORS EMPLOYED IN THE DECOR.

Opposite: BLENDING IN BEAUTIFULLY WITH A VARIETY OF DIVERSE FURNISHINGS AND STRONG ARCHITECTURAL COMPONENTS, A PARTNERS DESK WITH COLONIAL STYLING IS THE FOCAL POINT OF THIS RELATIVELY RELAXED OFFICE SPACE. THE PLACEMENT OF THE DESK IS ASTUTE, ALLOWING THE OCCUPANTS OF THE OFFICE EASY ACCESS TO THE BUILT-IN SHELVES. **Above:** TWO SIGNIFICANT STYLES ARE BLENDED SKILLFULLY AND SEAMLESSLY IN THIS FORMAL LIBRARY AND OFFICE SPACE WITH STUNNING RESULTS. THE NEOCLASSICAL ARCHITECTURAL DETAILS OF THE ROOM, SUCH AS THE DORIC COLUMNS AND THE GOUGEWORK PATTERN IN THE WAINSCOTING, ARE PURE EMPIRE, WHILE THE FURNISHINGS AND ACCESSORIES ARE PERFECT EXAMPLES OF ARTS AND CRAFTS DESIGN. THE SUCCESS OF THE DECOR IS OWED TO THE SIMPLICITY OF THE REST OF ITS EFFECTS, SUCH AS THE USE OF RECESSED LIGHTING INSTEAD OF FIXTURES AND SUBTLE MINIBLINDS INSTEAD OF FULL-BLOWN WINDOW TREATMENTS.

Below: THE QUAINT COLONIAL APPEAL OF THE DECOR EFFECTIVELY MASKS THE HIGHLY PRODUCTIVE NATURE OF THIS HOME OFFICE. A BANK OF BUILT-IN CABINETS EMBELLISHED WITH PERIOD TRIM INCORPORATES A DESK, LEAVING THE CENTER OF THE ROOM FREE FOR A LARGE PEDESTAL TABLE THAT CAN BE USED FOR MEETINGS OR COMMUNAL PROJECTS. FETCHING ACCENTS, SUCH AS DEEPLY HUED WALLS AND TIEBACK DRAPES, HELP COMPLETE THE CHARMING PICTURE.

Above: ONE OF THE BENEFITS OF WORKING AT HOME IS TAKING ADVANTAGE OF THE ENVIRONMENT'S ASSETS. HERE, A SECTION OF AN UNUSUALLY LARGE GREAT ROOM THAT BORDERS A BEAUTIFUL BACKYARD HAS BEEN CONVERTED INTO A PLEASANT HOME OFFICE THAT MAKES THE MOST OF THE HOME'S INTERIOR AND EXTERIOR ATTRIBUTES. A MASSIVE SHELVING UNIT TOPPED WITH TRIM THAT EMULATES MOLDING IS USED TO DEFINE THE OFFICE, WHILE DESKS DETAILED WITH TOUCHES OF CLASSICAL STYLING ARE PLACED END-TO-END TO FACE THE BACKYARD.

Opposite: A COMPROMISE WAS REACHED IN THIS TASTEFUL ROOM THAT TREADS A FINE LINE BETWEEN THE SEXES. THE IMPOSING TUFTED LEATHER SOFA IS ALL MALE, WHILE THE ELEGANT QUEEN ANNE DESK HAS A FAR MORE FEMININE SILHOUETTE. THE SPARE WHITE BUILT-INS AND PALE BLUE WALLS CREATE A NEUTRAL BACKDROP, WHICH IS ACCENTED BY ARTIFACTS THAT OFFER A BALANCE, SUCH AS HANDSOME ANTIQUE LEATHER-BOUND BOOKS AND FINE MEDITERRANEAN POTTERY.

Opposite: IN THIS STRIKING OFFICE, ELEGANCE AND GRANDEUR ARE BALANCED BY ECLECTIC ABANDON, ILLUSTRATING THAT TRADITIONAL TRAPPINGS ARE NOT ALWAYS TAME. FEDERAL AND EMPIRE STYLING, WITH THEIR NEOCLASSICAL MOTIFS, ARE STILL THE PREVALENT INFLUENCES EMPLOYED HERE, EVIDENT IN THE ARCHITECTURAL ELEMENTS AND MOST OF THE FURNISHINGS. BUT THIS OFFICE IS ALSO RIFE WITH FANTASTIC ODDITIES THAT ADD A WHIMSICAL SPIRIT TO THE SPACE. PIECES SUCH AS A FANCIFUL HORN CHAIR, A SPECTACULAR CHANDELIER, AND A HAND-PAINTED TURN-OF-THE-CENTURY LAMP IMMEDIATELY GRAB THE EYE AND SET A NEW STANDARD FOR THE ROOM.

Above: COLOR AND TONE ARE DEFTLY USED IN THIS EXQUISITE SETTING TO BOTH ENRICH AND OFFSET THE EFFECTS OF THE DARK WOODS. BEAUTIFUL ANTIQUE LEATHER BOOKS ARE BOUND IN LUXURIANT SHADES OF BLACK, RED, BROWN, AND GREEN, AND ARE HEAVILY EMBOSSED WITH RADIANT GOLD LEAF, A COLOR SCHEME THAT IS ECHOED THROUGHOUT THE ROOM. THE EMPIRE ARMCHAIR, THE DIRECTOIRE DESK, AN ELEGANT OIL, AN OPULENT THROW, AND EVEN A STUNNING TOPIARY POT ARE ALL GILT-ENCRUSTED, GLEAMING SEDUCTIVELY IN THE SETTING. **Right:** THE AMBIENCE INSPIRED BY A WILD ANIMAL THEME CAN BE CUNNINGLY CALLED UP WITHOUT ACTUALLY DISPLAYING ANYTHING THAT HAS BEEN STUFFED. HERE, AN INVENTIVE WINDOW TREATMENT TRICKS THE EYE BY CREATING THE IMAGE OF A POWERFUL LEOPARD'S HEAD, WHILE PIECES WITH LEOPARD PATTERNING ARE SKILLFULLY INTERSPERSED THROUGHOUT THE SPACE. THE REST OF THE ROOM'S APPOINTMENTS ARE TINGED WITH TINTS OF HONEY AND ACCENTED WITH TOUCHES OF BLACK, FURTHER REINFORCING THE MOTIF.

Opposite: THIS UNIQUE WORK SPACE IS THE PERFECT HAVEN FOR AN ADMIRER OF REGENCY AND EMPIRE STYLING. THE BREATH-TAKING BEAUTY OF A NEOCLASSICAL MOSAIC FLOOR, COUPLED WITH A COMFORTABLY CUSHIONED SEATING AREA CARVED OUT OF A SECLUDED CORNER, MAKES THE SPACE ENTICING, WHILE PERIOD FURNISHINGS COMPLETE THE PRETTY PICTURE. BUT THE EARTHY TONES OF THE TILE, COUPLED WITH THE COOL GREEN HUE ON THE WALLS, MAKES THE SPACE EXCEPTIONALLY CAPTIVATING.

Above: A CONTEMPORARY DWELLING CAN EASILY HARBOR A TRADITIONAL OFFICE WITH THE HELP OF THE RIGHT DECORATIVE DEVICES. GIVEN THE MODERNIST OVERTONES EVIDENT IN THE ARCHITECTURE, JAPONAISERIE STYLING MAKES A LOT OF SENSE FOR THIS ABODE. ALTHOUGH IT NEVER REACHED THE HEIGHTS OF CHINOISERIE, A CONSIDERABLE AMOUNT OF FURNITURE OF THIS ILK WAS STILL BEING MADE DURING THE NINETEENTH CENTURY. THIS DESK IS CLEARLY OF THAT PERIOD AND IS PERFECTLY PAIRED WITH FRENCH EMPIRE CHAIRS. A JAPANESE SCREEN MOUNTED ON THE WALL MAKES THE ORIENTAL EFFECT EVEN MORE PRONOUNCED.

Above: Two-person offices are often difficult to design, but the partners desk provides an engaging and equitable way to share space. Plus, it can be found, or fabricated, in virtually every variation, so it can be integrated into any decor. Here, an exquisite Federal-style version is the centerpiece of a carefully balanced room. An Empire ottoman and matching chairs mingle harmoniously with the contemporary pieces in the setting, thanks to the sophisticated use of texture and hue in the carpet and fabrics outfitting the room.

Right: An eclectic blend of furnishings from many eras can still impart a traditional effect. Here, an atypical mélange that makes the most of antiques works as a successful decor because all the pieces are relaxed and earthy, rather than elegant and refined. A Victorian reproduction of a Louis XVI armchair and a desk with Queen Anne styling are equally at home with a machine-age metal typing chair and a wicker and bamboo armoire. The neutral cream-colored backdrop also contributes to the success of the milieu, which manages to accommodate all sorts of high-tech equipment inconspicuously.

Left: REGAL PIECES OF PURE AMERICAN VICTORIANA ARE THE ULTIMATE IN TURN-OF-THE-CENTUTY STYLING. ALTHOUGH THESE PIECES DO NOT APPEAR IN A PERIOD SETTING, THEIR STRIKING PRESENCE GIVES THIS OFFICE A TRADITIONAL AIR. DEVOID OF ARCHITECTURAL DETAILING, THE EXPANSIVE ALL-WHITE ROOM ALLOWS THE BEAUTY OF EACH PIECE TO SHINE THROUGH.

Above: FORM MEETS FUNCTION IN THIS COMPACT CORNER WALL UNIT THAT EMBRACES PERIOD DESIGN. A COUNTRY THEME, WHICH BEGINS WITH THE PANELING AND WAINSCOTING OF THE ROOM, IS FINISHED OFF BY FABRICATING THE WALL UNIT FROM THE SAME KNOTTY PINE. BUT IT IS THE BURNISHED WOOD RATHER THAN PRONOUNCED ARCHITECTURAL DETAILING THAT GIVES THE UNIT, WHICH IS RELATIVELY UNEMBELLISHED, ITS DECORATIVE FLAIR.

CONTEMPORARY LINES

Sleek designs, gleaming surfaces, and basic, elementary lines are all characteristics that come to mind when talking about contemporary design. But the breadth of this decor is actually quite immense, encompassing far more than the simple traits we normally attribute to it. While a home office with contemporary styling can be stark and pristine, it can just as easily be warm and elegant, even whimsical.

Contemporary merely means "in the style of our times," and the furnishings that are being made today take their cues from a broad spectrum of influences. Modernism, the pivotal architectural style created just before World War I, came to embody "all things contemporary" by inspiring a pared-down approach to design. But it actually paved the way for many types of decor that have evolved since that time, which embrace—yet expand upon—the style's spare, refined lines.

Today it is rare to find a home entirely given over to any singular period of design. We pick and choose furnishings with little regard for a specific style, and eclectic blends that incorporate "a bit of this and some of that" seem to be the order of the day. So when it comes to contemporary design, there are no set rules. Sleekly styled furnishings can set a contemporary tone, or pieces from various periods and cultures can be used together in a groundbreaking way. Although the spectrum of "contemporary" design is quite wide, the overall look is essentially fresh and new.

Opposite: THROUGH THE SKILLFUL USE OF CONTRAST AND COLOR, THIS HIGHLY STYLED WORK SPACE PRODUCES A DYNAMIC EFFECT. WHITE TILES AND A SOFT GRAY HUE DEFINE THE WORK STATION'S BOUNDARIES, BUT AT THE SAME TIME BLEND IN WITH THE OTHER FURNISHINGS IN THE LARGE ROOM. WHIMSICAL ELEMENTS, SUCH AS A BRIGHT RED CHAIR AND A SEMICIRCULAR DESK, ARE IMAGINATIVE TOUCHES THAT ENHANCE RATHER THAN OVERWHELM THE DECOR. **Above:** THE SIMPLICITY OF THIS CONTEMPORARY OFFICE BELIES ITS ELEGANCE, WHICH IS EVIDENT IN THE UNDERSTATED BUT SUMPTUOUS PIECES USED TO APPOINT THE ROOM. THE BUILT-INS AND SOFA ARE REFINED BUT EXTREMELY SPARE, MAKING THEM PERFECT FOILS FOR THE MODERNIST TABLES AND ELOQUENT MIES VAN DER ROHE CHAIR.

Opposite: EVERYTHING IS SHARED EQUALLY IN THIS TWO-PERSON SPACE, THANKS TO THE PERFECT SYMMETRY OF THE DESK, SHELVES, AND STORAGE CABINETS. THE DRAMATIC WORK SURFACE IS AN INVENTIVE INTERPRETATION OF A PARTNERS DESK, WITH AN INGENIOUS INSET AT ONE END THAT CAN ACCOMMODATE ANOTHER CHAIR OR TWO FOR MEETINGS. WITH ITS VIBRANT GREEN HUE, THIS HIGHLY USEFUL LEDGE ALSO SERVES AS AN ENGAGING DECORATIVE ACCENT THAT LIVENS UP THE ROOM, MAKING IT A BRIGHTER, MORE PLEASANT ENVIRONMENT IN WHICH TO WORK. COORDINATING GREEN-TINTED GLASS PROVIDES AN ADDITIONAL SPLASH OF COLOR AND HIDES UNATTRACTIVE OFFICE SUPPLIES.

Above: THOUGH THIS HOME OFFICE IS ALMOST ENTIRELY PURE WHITE, IT IS ANYTHING BUT PRISSY AND IMPRACTICAL. THE COLOR CREATES A SLEEK LOOK, STREAMLINING THE VARIED AND POWERFUL ARCHITECTURAL COMPONENTS OF THE ROOM. NOW THE COMPLEX GEOMETRY OF THE WOOD JOIST CEILING SUBTLY BLENDS IN WITH THE SOFFIT USED FOR RECESSED LIGHTING, WHILE A HANDSOME BUT PROMINENT HEARTH IS TURNED INTO A GRACEFUL FOCAL POINT FOR THE ROOM.

Opposite: WHILE AN EXPANSE OF GLASS USUALLY EMPHASIZES THE ENVIRONMENT OUTDOORS, THE OBVIOUS COMFORT AND REFINEMENT OF THIS ROOM DRAWS THE EYE BACK INSIDE. A TASTEFUL BLEND OF CLASSICALLY STYLED YET CONTEMPORARY PIECES GIVES THE ROOM A WARM AND RESTFUL AIR. **Right:** THOUGH A SOOTHING PALETTE OF EARTH TONES MAKES THIS OFFICE SEEM SUBDUED, IT IS ACTUALLY QUITE UNCONVENTIONAL. SINGULAR PIECES OF FURNITURE, SUCH AS A FUNKY SET OF SUITCASES TURNED INTO A STORAGE CHEST, BRING ORIGINALITY AND WIT TO THIS INVENTIVE CONTEMPORARY SPACE. A WALL UNIT AND CHAIR SEEM MORE STANDARD AT FIRST GLANCE, BUT ACTUALLY ONLY EMULATE MORE TRADITIONAL DESIGNS. THE CHAIR MERELY INCORPORATES TOUCHES OF CLASSICAL STYLING, WHILE THE LINES OF THE CANTILEVERED SHELVES ARE UNDENIABLY DISTINCTIVE.

Below: THE ARCHITECTURAL STRUCTURE OF A ROOM CAN BECOME AN INTEGRAL ASPECT OF ITS DESIGN, AS EVIDENCED BY THIS SPECTACULAR HOME OFFICE. HERE, THE SLANTED CEILING OF AN ATTIC SERVES AS A SOLID ANCHOR FOR A BUILT-IN UNIT THAT AFFORDS THE AREA PLENTY OF STORAGE AND AN INGENIOUS TWO-PERSON WORK SURFACE. CABINETS AND DRAWERS ARE CARVED OUT OF THE SNUG CAVITY CREATED BY THE PITCH OF THE CEILING, WHICH WOULD NORMALLY BE DEAD SPACE. THE SUBDUED TONES OF THE "TWO-TIERED" FLOOR TREATMENT WORK WELL WITH THE SIMPLE WHITES AND BLACKS EMPLOYED IN THE REST OF THE ROOM. **Opposite:** BASIC FURNISHINGS BECOME ENGAGING AND BOLD WITH THE RIGHT KIND OF ACCESSORIES TO ACCENTUATE THEM. HERE, PLAIN CONTEMPORARY PIECES WITH BLACK WOOD VENEERS RECEIVE CHARACTER FROM AN ANTIQUE DRESS FORM, FRESH FLOWERS, AND A WARM WOODEN DESK CHAIR WITH VINTAGE STYLING. INTERESTING LIGHTING ALSO JAZZES UP THE SPACE: A SLEEK TASK LAMP IS FOCUSED ON THE DESKTOP, WHILE A SCULPTURAL SPOTLIGHT ILLUMINATES THE REST OF THE ROOM.

Above: BLACK, THE COLOR SYMBOLICALLY ASSOCIATED WITH "THE ABSOLUTE," MAKES AN UNEQUIVOCAL IMPRESSION IN A ROOM. THIS STRIKING OFFICE EXUDES STRENGTH AND OFFERS AN EXTREMELY EFFICIENT ENVIRONMENT. ITS RESOURCEFUL FLOOR PLAN MAKES THE MOST OF EVERY SQUARE FOOT, WHILE THE SLEEK, DARK APPOINTMENTS SET A COMMANDING TONE.

Left: IF BUILT-INS ARE OUT OF THE QUESTION, SIMPLE MODULAR UNITS CAN BE USED TO CREATE A CLEAN, CONTEMPORARY WORK SPACE IN ANY ROOM. THE UP-TO-DATE DESIGN OF THIS SYSTEM EASILY ACCOMMODATES COMPUTER EQUIPMENT AND TAKES ERGONOMICS INTO ACCOUNT, MAKING IT AN EFFECTIVE OPTION FOR CREATING A HOME OFFICE. PLUS, ITS NEUTRAL LINES CAN JIBE WITH A WIDE RANGE OF DECORATIVE STYLES. **Above:** FURNISHINGS WITH MODERNIST STYLING ARE USED TO DEFINE AN OFFICE IN A MIES VAN DER ROHE APARTMENT, SINCE THE SPACE HAS BEEN RESTORED TO ITS ORIGINAL STATE AND IS DEVOID OF ALL WALLS. THE SIMPLICITY OF THE SETTING, WHICH IS FURTHER AFFIRMED BY THE USE OF A NEUTRAL PALETTE AND A DISCIPLINED LACK OF ACCESSORIES, ALLOWS THE INTRINSIC BEAUTY OF THE EXQUISITELY CRAFTED WOOD PIECES TO SHINE THROUGH.

Below: A RICHLY HUED, VARIEGATED PAINT JOB ADDS WARMTH TO THE PURE CONTEMPORARY LINES OF THE PIECES IN THIS ROOM AND MAKES A MAGNIFICENT BACKDROP FOR A COLLECTION OF PRE-COLUMBIAN ARTIFACTS. THOUGH THE HEAVILY GLAZED WALLS WERE ACTUALLY INTENDED TO COORDINATE WITH THE OPULENT BIRD'S-EYE MAPLE OF THE DESK AND CREDENZA, THEY ALSO MAKE THE ROOM MUCH WARMER. LOW-VOLTAGE LIGHTING DRAWS ATTENTION TO THE MOST DRAMATIC COMPONENTS OF THE SPACE—A STUNNING SYSTEM OF CANTILEVERED GLASS SHELVES AND A SLEEK FIREPLACE. **Opposite:** THROUGH THE USE OF DYNAMIC ARCHITECTURAL COMPONENTS AND CLASSIC MODERN FURNISHINGS, THIS HUGE ATTIC HAS BEEN CONVERTED INTO A SPARE BUT FASHIONABLE HOME OFFICE. A STREAMLINED SKYLIGHT AND AN UNUSUAL PICTURE WINDOW WITH A GLASS PEDIMENT EMPHASIZE THE UNIQUE BEAUTY OF THE ROOM'S STRUCTURAL "BONES," WHILE SIMPLE BUILT-INS TEAMED WITH MARCEL BREUER'S WASSILY CHAIRS ADD A COMPLEMENTARY DECORATIVE FLAIR.

Above: CHARMING ANTIQUE PIECES LEND PANACHE TO A RELATIVELY ROUTINE SET OF PLAIN WHITE SHELVES. TOGETHER THE FURNISHINGS CREATE AN INTERESTING OFFICE AREA, WHICH STILL RETAINS A CONTEMPORARY FEEL THANKS TO THE ABUNDANT LIGHTING AND CRISP TONES OF THE SETTING.

Left: THERE ARE LESSONS TO BE LEARNED FROM AN ARCHITECT'S APPROACH TO SETTING UP A CONTEMPORARY HOME OFFICE IN A VINTAGE LOFT. AN IMMENSE DESK IS ASYMMETRICALLY ALIGNED AT ONE END OF THE EXPANSIVE SPACE, CREATING AN AVANT-GARDE YET EXTREMELY EFFICIENT LAYOUT. THANKS TO ITS POSITIONING, THE DESK PROVIDES ITS OCCUPANT WITH TWO SPECIFIC TASK AREAS. **Above:** JUST A FEW SLEEK PIECES CAN HAVE A POWERFUL EFFECT IN A HOME OFFICE. DESPITE THE PROSAIC BACKDROP OF THIS ROOM, A SCULPTURAL DESK AND DEBONAIR CHAIR ADD SPIRIT AND SPUNK TO THE SETTING. THE COOL, CLEAN HUES EMPLOYED IN THE MILIEU KEEP THE MOOD DIGNIFIED AND FOCUSED ON BUSINESS.

Above: THIS OPEN EXPANSE IN A SOARING ATTIC HAS BEEN MADE INTIMATE BY BREAKING UP THE SPACE INTO SMALLER, AND DECORATIVELY DISTINCT, SETTINGS. CAREFREE WICKER CREATES A BREEZY CORNER ON ONE SIDE OF THE ROOM, WHILE MORE TRADITIONAL TRAPPINGS ARE STRATEGICALLY ARRANGED TO CARVE OUT A SERIOUS HOME OFFICE RIGHT ALONGSIDE. **Right:** THE PROFESSIONAL LOOK OF THIS TWO-PERSON SPACE WAS ACHIEVED WITH COMMERCIAL FURNISHINGS ACCENTED BY MINIMAL BUT POWERFUL PIECES OF ART. GRASSCLOTH WALLPAPER AND MATCHSTICK BLINDS IN MELLOW TONES SOFTEN THE SPACE, WHILE EYE-CATCHING COWHIDE DESK CHAIRS ADD A FANCIFUL TOUCH.

Sources

(page 74)
Michael Lehrer, architect
Lehrer Architects
Los Angeles, CA
(213) 664-4747

Joanne Belsen, designer
Los Angeles, CA
(213) 654-3253

(page 75)
James Gillan, architect
San Francisco, CA
(415) 398-1120

(pages 76 right, 269)
Van Martin-Rowe
Los Angeles, CA
(818) 577-4736

(page 78)
Margot Alofsin
Los Angeles, CA
(310) 395-8008

(page 79)
Biben/Busley
Biben/Busley Architects
Claremont, CA
(909) 624-8601

(page 84)
Jefferson Riley, architect
Centerbrook Architects
Essex, CT
(860) 767-0175

(page 85)
Florence Perchuk, CKD
St. Charles Kitchens of New
York
New York, NY
(212) 838-2812

(page 88 right)
John B. Scholz, architect
Scholz & Barclay Architects
Camden, ME
(207) 236-0777

(page 92)
John Silverio
Lincolnville, ME
(207) 763-3885

(page 96)
Cann & Company
Boston, MA
(617) 338-8814

(page 97)
Carole Hanson
White House Farm
Foster, RI
(401) 397-4386

(page 102)
Bruce Bierman Design
New York, NY
(212) 243-1935

(pages 106 right, 190)
Larry Totah
Totah Design
Los Angeles, CA
(213) 653-0416

(page 106 left)
Joe Matta, designer
Masterwork Kitchens
Goshen, NY
(914) 294-9792

(page 108)
Lynette Hand
F. Kia-The Store
Boston, MA
(617) 357-5553

(page 109)
Centerbrook Architects
Essex, CT
(860) 767-0175

(page 111)
Scott Marble and Karen
Fairbanks Architects
New York, NY
(212) 233-0653

(page 112)
Mark Rios
Rios Associates Inc.
Los Angeles, CA
(213) 852-6717

(page 117 top)
John D. Morris II
Architects/Land Planners
Camden, ME
(207) 236-8321

(page 117 right)
Kuckly Associates
New York, NY
(212) 722-2888

(page 123)
Osburn Design
San Francisco, CA
(415) 487-2333

(page 124 right)
Lesley Achitoff
No Fo Decorative Painting and
Plastering
New York, NY
(212) 807-0546

Karina Werner-Jakobi
Jakobi Studio
New York, NY
(212) 977-5142

(page 124 left)
Antique Stove Heaven
Los Angeles, CA
(323) 298-5581

(page 126)
Candra Scott
San Francisco, CA
(415) 861-0690

(page 132)
Dewing & Schmid Architects
Cambridge, MA
(617) 876-0066

(pages 133, 137)
Mary Drysdale
Drysdale Design Associates
Inc.
Washington, D.C.
(202) 588-0700

(page 135)
Douglas Truesdale Interior
Design
Boston, MA
(617) 338-1156

(page 139)
Edward Kozanlian, architect
New York, NY
(212) 838-4438

(page 141)
Barbara Barry Inc.
Los Angeles, CA
(310) 276-9977

(page 150)
Hutton Wilkinson
Los Angeles, CA
(213) 874-7760

(page 152)
Robert Curry
New York, NY
(212) 206-0505

(pages 154, 170, 179 left,
187, 207)
Jarret Hedborg
Wall paintings by Nancy
Kinisch
Los Angeles, CA
(310) 271-1437

(page 155)
François Theise
Adesso Furniture
Boston, MA
(617) 451-2212

(page 156)
Roy McMakin
Seattle, WA
(206) 323-6992

(pages 157, 176)
Denise Domergue
Los Angeles, CA
(310) 453-7717

(page 158)
Heidi Wianecki
Los Angeles, CA
(310) 459-5550

(page 159)
Janet Schirn Design Group
Chicago, IL
(312) 222-0017

(pages 160 top, 209)
Tessa Kennedy
London, England
071 221 4546

(page 160 bottom)
Tom Callaway

Los Angeles, CA
(310) 828-1030

(page 161)
Goodman/Charlton
Los Angeles, CA
(310) 657-7068

(page 162)
John Kulhanek
Los Angeles, CA
(310) 474-6722

(page 163)
Diane Thompson
Modern Living
Los Angeles, CA
(213) 655-3898

(page 165)
Joel Chen
Los Angeles, CA
(213) 655-6310

(pages 166 bottom, 196)
Tanys Langdon, architect
Chicago, IL
(312) 282-2144

(page 174)
Barbara Barry
Los Angeles, CA
(310) 276-9977

(page 175)
Janice McCarthy
Los Angeles, CA
(213) 651-4229

(page 177 left)
Tom Catalano
Boston, MA
(617) 338-6447

(page 181)
Peter Bohlin, architect
Philadelphia, PA
(215) 592-0600

(page 182)
Anita Calero
New York, NY
(212) 727-8949

(pages 183, 272)
Richar Interiors
Chicago, IL
(312) 951-0924

(pages 184, 237)
Charles Riley
New York, NY
(212) 206-8395

(page 186)
John Gillespie, architect
Camden, MN
(207) 236-8054

(page 188 right)
Lindsay Boutrous-Ghali
Lindsay Associates
Boston, MA
(617) 262-1948

(page 189)
Bob Knight, architect
Blue Hill, MN
(207) 374-2845

(page 191)
Reiter & Reiter
Boston, MA
(617) 965-0289

(page 192)
C & J Katz Studio
Boston, MA
(617) 367-0537

(pages 194, 214, 236, 242,
270)
Herman Miller for the Home
Zeeland, MI
(800) 646-4400

(page 197 right)
Tom Bosworth
Seattle, WA
(206) 522-5549

(page 199)
Laura Clayton Baker
Los Angeles, CA
(310) 573-1232

(page 200)
Penny Bianchi
Los Angeles, CA
(213) 682-1487

(page 201)
Sarah Kaltman
New York, NY
(212) 721-6497

(page 203)
Annie Kelly
Los Angeles, CA
(213) 876-8030

(page 206 left)
Michel Pouliot, artist
Dorchester, MA
(617) 265-7576

(pages 206, 231)
Peter Wheeler
P.J. Wheeler and Associates
Boston, MA
(617) 426-5921

(page 210)
Patricia O'Shaunesey
New York, NY
(212) 674-2833

(page 218)
Anne Lenox
Partners in Design
Newton Center, MA
(617) 969-3626

(page 219)
Jan Tomlinson
Trophy Club, TX
(817) 491-9628

(page 221)
Walter Chatham Architects
New York, NY
(212) 925-2202

(page 222)
Keith Hone
Pennington, NJ
(609) 513-7260

(page 226)
Cathy Morehead and
Associates
Santa Ana, CA
(714) 542-6504

(page 228)
Mark Stumer, designer
Peter Johns, assistant designer
Mojo-Stumer Associates
Roslyn, NY
(516) 625-3344

(page 230)
Scott Brownell, architect
Newport Beach, CA
(714) 548-6522

(page 233)
Audio/Video Interiors
Woodland Hills, CA
(818) 593-3923

(page 237)
Maxine Ordesky
Organized Designs
Beverly Hills, CA
(310) 277-0499

(page 238)
Anna Belle Marshall, CKD.
Valley Concepts and Design
Lake Forest, CA
(714) 951-7898

(page 239 right)
J.P. Franzen Associates, architects
Southport, CT
(203) 259-0529

(page 239 left)
Kenneth Solomon, designer
KJS Interiors, Ltd.
Glen Head, NY
(516) 759-4500

(page 243)
Charlotte Moss, designer
Charlotte Moss & Co.
New York, NY
(212) 772-6244

(page 245)
Mariette Himes, ASID
Gomez Associates
New York, NY
(212) 288-6856

(pages 248, 257)
Joseph L. Roman, ASID
Wainscott, NY
(516) 324-5763

(page 250)
Barbara Winslow, partner in
charge of design
Jacobson Silverstein Winslow,
Architects
Berkeley, CA
(510) 848-8861

(page 251)
Tim Button, designer
Stedila Design, Inc.
New York, NY
(212) 865-6611

(page 255)
Vince Lattuca
New York, NY
(212) 758-2720

(page 256)
Gail Green Interior Design
New York, NY
(212) 980-1098

(pages 258, 267 left)
Celeste Cooper
The Cooper Group
Boston, MA
(617) 426-3865

(page 261)
Judi Cunningham
Chez Joli
Winnetka, IL
(708) 446-2522

(page 264)
Blair Ballard and Associates
Laguna Beach, CA
(714) 494-8093

(page 266)
Siegel & Strain
Emeryville, CA
(510) 547-8092

(page 268)
Interior Consultants
Salem, NY
(914) 533-2275

(page 271)
Powell/Kleinschmidt
Chicago, IL
(312) 642-6450

(page 274)
Charles Damga, designer
Damga Design
New York, NY
(212) 570-1439

(page 276)
Ginsburg Development
Corporation
Hawthorne, NY
(914) 747-3600

PHOTOGRAPHY CREDITS

©William Abranowitz: 217, 254 left

©Phillip Beaurline: 224 right, 232

©Judith Bromley: 166 bottom, 168, 196

Arcaid: ©Richard Bryant: 29, 58 left, 61 right; ©Annet Held: 202 top; ©Simon Kelly/Belle: 38, 110 (architects: P. Stronach/T. Allison); ©Willem Rethmeier/Belle: 105 bottom (design: George Freedman)

©Jean Wright: 208 (architect: Deece Giles, Sidney, Australia)

Crandall and Crandall Associates: ©Knopf: 226, ©Pallette: 230 left, ©Oldham: 238, ©Neimann: 264

©Daniel Eifert: 248 (design: Joseph L/ Roman), 257

©Phillip Ennis Photography: 19, 32 left, 60, 228 left (design: Mojo Stumer Associates), 233 (design: Audio/Video Interiors), 234 left, 239 right (design: KJS Interiors), 241, 244-245 (design: Mariette Himes, ASID, Gomez Associates), 256 (design: Gail Green Interior Design), 267

©Esto Photographics: ©Peter Aaron: 271 right;

©Otto Baitz: 227 left, 252 left, 273; ©Mark Darley: 223 right, 225, 250, 266; ©Scott Frances: 221, 252 right; ©Jeff Goldberg: 216, 224 left

©Feliciano: 22, 35

©Tony Giammarino: 102, 140 left (Bruce Bierman Design, Inc.), 144 right

©Tria Giovan: 6, 26, 28, 30, 31 right, 39, 44, 67, 182 left, 184-185, 201, 210, 230 right, 246, 249 right, 263

©Rob Gray: 120 left (decorative painter: Lesley Achitoff-Gray, design: Karina Werner-Jakobi), 139 (architect: Ed Kozanlian)

©Steve Gross & Susan Daley: 101, 130, 138, 140 right

©Nancy Hill: 23, 47, 51, 68, 72 left

©image/dennis krukowski: 85 (design: Florence Perchuk, CKD), 128 bottom (design Gail Pearlman, I.S.I.D.)

©The Interior Archive: ©Ari Ashley: 91, 121; ©Tim Beddow: 98 right, 122, 128 top; ©Simon Brown: 104, 105 top; ©J. Pilkington: 93; ©James Mortimer: 94, 95, 118; ©Jakob Wastgerg: 144 left; ©Henry Wilson: 120 right, 143 right

©Jennifer Levy: 222 (design: Keith Hone), 227 left (design: Maxine Ordesky), 237 right

©David Livingston: 14, 24, 25, 32 right, 46 right, 48, 52, 53, 54, 55 left, 57, 62 left, 64 left, 64-65, 69, 71, 75, 90, 112 left, 116, 123 (Osburn Design), 124, 126 (design: Candra Scott Associates), 171

©Richard Mandelkorn: 188 bottom, 251 (Stedila Design, Inc.), 258 left (design: Celeste Cooper), 268 left

©Maura McEvoy: 82, 106 left (design: Joe Matta for Masterwork Kitchens, countertops design: Steven Eickelbeck), 113 (design: Bennett Bean)

Courtesy of Herman Miller, Inc./©Nick Merrick/ Hedrich Blessing: 194-195, 214, 236, 242-243, 270-271

©Michael Mundy: 2, 40-41, 41 right, 46 left, 61 left, 164, 166 top, 172, 173

©Mary Nichols: 159

©Peter Paige: 111 (design: Marble Fairbanks), 274-275 (Damga Design)

©Robert Perron: 239 left (design: J.P. Franzen Associates)

©David Phelps: 17, 36, 43, 73 top, 132 top (courtesy of *American Homestyle & Gardening* Magazine), 179 bottom, 182 right, 202 bottom, 237 right (design: Charles Riley, courtesy of *Woman's Day* Magazine), 269 (design: Van Martin-Rowe)

Courtesy of Richar Interiors/©James Yochum: 183, 272 right

©Eric Roth: 20, 66, 89 (design: Elizabeth Speert, Inc.), 96 (design: Cann & Company), 97 (design: Carole Hanson), 108 (design: Lynn Hand), 117 bottom (designer: Kuckly Associates, Inc.), 132 bottom (architects: Dewing & Schmid), 135 (design: Geib Truesdale Interior Design), 155, 180, 192, 193, 198 top, 206 top, 206 bottom, 218 (design: Anne Lenox, Partners in Design), 231 (design: Peter Wheeler), 240, 253

©Bill Rothchild: 243 right (design: Charlotte Moss & Company), 255 (design: Vince Latucca), 268 right (design: Interior /Consultants), 276 left (design: Ginsburg Development Corporation)

©Tim Street-Porter: 5, 13, 27